Hope!

This Book is the
Property of the Retreat

Other Titles by Dick B.

Dr. Bob and His Library: Books for Twelve Step Growth
Anne Smith's Journal, 1933-1939: A.A.'s Principles of Success
*The Oxford Group and Alcoholics Anonymous: A Design for
  Living That Works*
The Akron Genesis of Alcoholics Anonymous
New Light on Alcoholism: God, Sam Shoemaker, and A.A.
The Books Early AAs Read for Spiritual Growth
Courage to Change (with Bill Pittman)
The Good Book and The Big Book: A.A.'s Roots in the Bible
*That Amazing Grace: The Role of Clarence and Grace S. in
  Alcoholics Anonymous*
*Good Morning!: Quiet Time, Morning Watch, Meditation, and
  Early A.A.*
*Turning Point: A History of Early A.A.'s Spiritual Roots and
  Successes*
Utilizing Early A.A.'s Spiritual Roots for Recovery Today
The Golden Text of A.A.: God, the Pioneers, and Real Spirituality
*By the Power of God: A Guide to Early A.A. Groups & Forming
  Similar Groups Today*
*Making Known the Biblical History and Roots of Alcoholics
  Anonymous: An Eleven-Year Research, Writing, Publishing, and
  Fact Dissemination Project*
*Why Early A.A. Succeeded: The Good Book in Alcoholics
  Anonymous Yesterday and Today (A Bible Study Primer for AAs
  and other 12-Steppers)*
God and Alcoholism: Our Growing Opportunity in the 21st Century

Hope!

The Story of Geraldine Owen Delaney, Alina Lodge & Recovery

Dick B.

Tincture of Time Press
Kihei, Hawaii

Tincture of Time Press, Box 837, Kihei, HI 96753-0837

Tincture of Time Press is a division of Paradise Research
Publications, Inc., Box 837, Kihei, HI 96753-0837

Cover Design: Lili Crawford (Maui Cyber Design)

The publication of this volume does not imply affiliation with nor
approval or endorsement from Alcoholics Anonymous World
Services, Inc.

Publisher's Cataloging in Publication

B., Dick.
      Hope! : the story of Geraldine D., Alina Lodge & Recovery/ by
      Dick B. -- 2d ed.
      p. cm.
      Includes bibliographical references and index.
      ISBN: 1-885803-33-8

      1. D., Geraldine, 1907- 2. Alcoholics Anonymous--Biography. 3.
      Little Hill-Alina Lodge (N.J.) 4. Alcoholics--United States--
      Biography. I. Title.

HV5293.D22B23 2002   362.29'286'092

To the Mom whose dream it was to create a book which would record the story of Mrs. Geraldine O. Delaney; provide the details as to how Mrs. Delaney's Alina Lodge became established; explain some of the vital elements which contributed (and today still contribute) to its success; and point up the unique significance of Mrs. D., the Little Hill Alina Lodge; and their non-permissive recovery program as sources of hope today to suffering alcoholics and their families.

She wrote the chapter called "Mom." "Alex" is about her son's experiences as a student at Alina Lodge.

Contents

Acknowledgments

In his research prior to writing the First Edition of this title, the author was warmly welcomed at Little Hill-Alina Lodge by Mrs. Geraldine Delaney. She arranged for every need to be met, looked after his personal welfare, saw to it that he had access to staff, operations, buildings, and memorabilia. She also fully and frankly answered every question she was asked.

In order to preserve anonymity, fictitious names were used throughout the book (except for Mrs. Delaney's full name in this Second Edition, and the name of her successor Mark Schottinger). The use of fictitious names was and is consistent with A.A.'s Twelve Traditions. People connected with the Lodge may well recognize the personalities, but the author thought it best to preserve the anonymity of the former and present staff, parent, and former student with whom interviews were conducted. The Lodge personnel were helpful and provided interviews and written materials.

I again thank my son Ken. Ken is a computer specialist, Bible scholar, church pastor, and friend. A good part of his life has been spent helping me with all phases of my research, writing, publication, and distribution. Nothing would have been possible without Ken's patient, astute help!

Foreword

Geraldine O. Delaney's initials—G.O.D.—indicate to one and all the source of gigantic strength of body and soul that enabled her to do the Herculean work the dear Lord asked her to do for the shattered souls to whom she dedicated her life.

Having been liberated from the prison of alcoholism which had brought her to the gate of death, she gratefully plunged into the work of freeing others from the same prison. She founded Alina Lodge and created a Therapy of Education for her "students" in a regime of iron discipline she believed to be essential in treating those characterized as being "self-will run riot" into normal people dedicated to the well-being of others, as voiced by the 12th Step of AA, the basic therapy for alcoholics. She explained to all patients during their orientation classes that they had created every rule at the Lodge. However, it must be understood that what made her and her beloved Alina Lodge so successful was her deeply passionate love of alcoholics.

I met Mrs. Delaney 25 or so years ago and was deeply impressed by the simplicity of the treatment she had set up, but above all by her total commitment to her students. My admiration has grown over the years. Her approval of the things I've done has been one of the greatest rewards of my life.

I whole heartedly approve and endorse this tribute to her life. The title, "HOPE," is a very accurate one indeed, for she gave such hope to so many "hopeless" souls.

Finally, a tiny peek into her own soul. A priest, a friend of many years of both hers and mine, entered the portals of Alina Lodge for long term treatment. During his first days there, he asked if he could attend Sunday Mass at a local parish. Her response: "God's not ready for you yet!" This man became a follower of hers and walked in her footsteps, dedicating the rest of his life to alcoholics, working in the field for many years unto his death.

Read these pages to be inspired by the life of an amazingly remarkable woman.

Father Joseph C. Martin, S.S.

[Father Martin is a Co-founder and President of Father Martin's Ashley, a private non-profit corporation, established in 1983. Ashley's is a treatment center for alcoholism and chemical addiction at Havre de Grace, Maryland. Father Martin is a noted speaker and author and is well-known for his "chalk talk" films—seen by patients at most treatment centers in America.]

1

Mrs. Delaney—The Lodge—Recovery

Stories

There are "drunkalogs" aplenty in Alcoholics Anonymous, in Twelve Step programs, and in "self-help" groups today. Suffering alcoholics and speakers trying to deal with life-controlling problems dote on "sharing experiences" involving their misdeeds, excesses, and miseries. Some stories have the commendable objective of helping others by sharing messages of "experience, strength, and hope."

Almost every conceivable 12-Step meeting has some kind of speaker, telling some kind of story, with some kind of purpose. Sometimes, the speaker's purpose seems to be just plain entertaining the audience; sometimes, to inspire them; sometimes, to establish with seemingly hopeless victims a sense of "belonging;" and sometimes to offer those who have ventured in, and committed their all, an assurance of worthwhile recovery.

Today's "alkies" love stories, and I was no exception. In fact, I found that, like so many other groups, Alcoholics Anonymous groups even had their own recognizable, special words and phrases. You knew when you were talking or listening to an A.A. member. It didn't matter whether you asked if he or she were a "friend of

Bill W." Or if you heard the suggestion, "turn it over." Or if you were exposed to words like "acceptance," a "god" of your own understanding, "willingness," "service," "higher power," or hundreds of others. If you were serious about recovery, as so many are, and as I was, you went to meeting after meeting, heard story after story, and listened to expression after expression that caught your attention. Probably, for a time at least, the language produced your loyalty to the ideas conveyed. In fact, you found yourself talking the same talk.

More often than not, particularly today, the stories have little to do with A.A.'s unusual, original, "spiritual" program of recovery–a program said to have been borrowed primarily from medicine, religion, and the experience of alcoholics. A.A.'s "story" concept came largely from A.A.'s initial parent fellowship–the Oxford Group–where good, old-fashioned "testimonies" and "testimonials" were called "sharing" or "witnessing." They were the heart of most meetings. Those stories were meant to convince listeners that our Creator, Yahweh, had done for the speaker or writer what he or she could not do for himself And early A.A. bought that idea (See, for example, *Alcoholics Anonymous*, 1st ed., New York: Works Publishing Company, 1939, pp. 20-21, 69, 96, 193, 216, 273, 379, 390).

As to the early days, however, A.A. Co-founder Dr. Bob commented in his last major address:

> Our stories didn't amount to anything to speak of. When we started in on Bill D. [A.A. Number Three], we had no Twelve Steps, either; we had no Traditions. But we were convinced that the answer to our problems was in the Good Book. . . . We already had the basic ideas, though not in terse and tangible form. We got them, as I said, as a result of our study of the Good Book (*The Co-Founders of Alcoholics Anonymous: Biographical sketches Their Last Major Talks*. New York: Alcoholics Anonymous World Services, Inc., 1972, 1975, pp. 13, 14. See also Dick B., *The Good Book and The Big Book*:

> *A.A.'s Roots in the Bible*, 3rd ed. HI: Paradise Research
> Publications, Inc., 1998).

A.A. Co-founder Bill Wilson pointed to A.A.'s other major
spiritual source, which was based on the Bible, but was a *fellowship*
of believers. This fellowship, called the Oxford Group, took its
principles and practices from the Bible. But its life-changing
program encompassed a great deal more than stories and sharing.
Thus Bill wrote:

> Where did the early AAs find the material for the remaining ten
> Steps? Where did we learn about moral inventory, amends for
> harms done, turning wills and lives over to God? Where did we
> learn about meditation and prayer and all the rest of it? The
> spiritual substance of our remaining ten Steps came straight
> from Dr. Bob's and my own earlier association with the Oxford
> Groups. . . (*The Language of the Heart*. New York: The AA
> Grapevine, Inc., 1988, p. 298. See also Dick B., *The Oxford
> Group and Alcoholics Anonymous: A Design for Living That
> Works*, 2d ed. HI: Paradise Research Publications, Inc., 1998).

When I spent a week interviewing Mrs. Delaney and preparing the
first edition of this book, I found her (at 90 years of age) eager to
talk about A.A. history, A.A.'s spiritual roots, and the materials I
had assembled to document them. And–for a very simple reason–she
knew quite well that the basics in the A.A. program were not about
stories. They were about a recovery *program*. A program that had
evolved--piece by piece--from the pioneers' study of the Bible,
prayer and meditation, reading religious literature, learning the
principles and practices of the Oxford Group, and hearing the
written and other ideas of Dr. Bob's wife Anne Smith (See Dick B.,
*Turning Point: A History of the Spiritual Roots and Successes of
Early A.A.* HI: Paradise Research Publications, Inc., 1998).
　　Now–and oddly, several years after Mrs. Delaney's death and
after completion of my first biography of her–I believe I better
understand one of the major principles Mrs. D. implanted at her

Alina Lodge. Many in today's A.A. are scared to death to mention or applaud "teaching," "thinking," or "studying anything but A.A. literature." The Lodge, however, is not so sterile. It insists on teaching, thinking, learning, and studying. It is not bereft of many kinds of reading material–so long as they don't divert from the Lodge program. For Geraldine Delaney knew perfectly well that Alcoholics Anonymous itself and the name of its principal book *Alcoholics Anonymous* came from "book larnin"–including what daily study of the Bible, various daily Bible devotionals, and many many religious books contained. All were read and circulated among A.A. pioneers. And Mrs. Delaney also knew that Bill Wilson had begun as early as 1938 selling the idea of an A.A. "textbook" which would contain the principles, practices, *and* applicable personal success stories that involved A.A.'s recovery *program.*

Mrs. Delaney called the residents (or patients, if you choose) at Alina Lodge "students." They were there, she believed, to read, to listen, to study, and to learn–not merely to tell stories or share failure experiences. But were there "stories" at Alina Lodge?

There sure were. Regular A.A. meetings and other fellowship meetings were (and are) held there for students to attend. The speakers told stories. Staff members shared their experiences. When I was there researching, I was invited to tell "my" story; and I did. And, though we'll speak much about Mrs. Delaney's ideas, program, and recovery achievements, we'll call your attention right now to her *story.* The story in the next chapter. The Geraldine Delaney story has been presented almost exactly as she told it–at the Lodge, at professional gatherings, at A.A. Conferences and Conventions, and at meetings.

She was an AA alright. You can see and hear it in her language, and her "students" could recognize her as one of their own! In fact, they were urged to move into A.A. upon their recovery and departure. And they were urged by one of the early women pioneers of A.A.–Geraldine O. Delaney.

The Delaney Touch

What we wrote in the first edition has changed little in content. Only in tense. Geraldine O. Delaney is dead. But her characteristics, her theories, and her accomplishments live on and still challenge students and staff and still produce victories over alcoholism. Here's how we commenced our first edition a few years ago:

She *was* "THE BOSS." Her chair cushion said so. At least two of her coffee mugs said so. And in the nurse's station at the rehabilitation center hangs this sign:

RULE 1: The boss is always right.
RULE 2: If the boss is wrong, refer to Rule 1.

There's more! Her New Jersey license plate had but one letter—"D." Her parking stall was marked "DO NOT EVEN THINK OF PARKING HERE." The name "Grambo," by which she was sometimes called, and sometimes called herself, was a relic of the Sylvester Stallone "Rambo" era. Mrs. D.'s cortege adapted the special name for her--taking that of the ferocious "Rambo" and adding a prefix connoting "Grandma." Hence, Grambo!

All of which seemed very clearly, and by intent, to convey the idea that this momma was tough. It also proclaimed others' perception of Mrs. Geraldine D. Ironically, the three initials for her full names spelled out G. O. D. They also stood for "Good Orderly Direction"—a doctrine she passionately believed in; and which she claimed was essential for recovery at the highly successful Little Hill-Alina Lodge rehabilitation program for alcoholics, poly addicted people, and their families. There was even a pointed saying among her peers about the Delaney touch and direction. It was to the effect that if addicts or alcoholics have failed in every other program, "Send them to Alina Lodge!" For Alina Lodge is a long-term treatment program designed to produce permanent recovery and a changed life for those "reluctant to recover" who complete its program.

Now just who *was* this seemingly autocratic lady?

When I met her shortly before her death, she had reached *ninety years of age, achieved seventy years of self-supporting employment, racked up fifty years of sobriety,* and *maintained some forty years of legendary association with Little Hill-Alina Lodge.* These things were made very real to me as I talked to her, examined her premises, and attended her programs. At 90, she was alert, caring, and inquiring. Though she had "retired" as head of the Lodge, she had an office right there, sat with staff at the table, and kept a watchful and guiding eye on activities. I heard her lead singing, speak to students, and confer with staff. She was the founder and had become, at that point, C.E.O. "Emeritus."

Here are some introductory details: For openers, A.A. co-founder Bill Wilson and his wife Lois (who was co-founder of Al-Anon) were her good friends; and Geraldine Delaney was one of the earliest A.A. women in the State of New Jersey (See *Women Pioneers In 12 Step Recovery.* MN: Hazelden Pittman Archives Press, 1999, pp. 158-65; *Pioneers We Have Known in the Field of Alcoholism.* Christopher D. Smithers Foundation, Limited Edition, pp. 57-58). The aforementioned names for Geraldine Owen Delaney probably epitomize her philosophy of long-term, non-permissive, discipline-oriented, structured-living as essential to recovery from alcoholism and other addictions. Perhaps the names are also indicative of the fact that this lady was, to the end, very much in charge of her own life and her own philosophy for successful treatment. She blazed a trail not soon to be forgotten.

Mrs. D. was usually called by her full last name, Delaney. Her friends frequently call her "Gerry." Others did occasionally refer to her as "Grambo" and, yes, "God." Whatever she was called, Mrs. Delaney qualifies as one of the earliest women members of Alcoholics Anonymous—a fellowship where women members were not particularly popular in the pioneer days. She was an avant-garde worker with women alcoholics. She herself was a pioneer in the no-

nonsense treatment of all addiction as a family disease. The "Lodge," which is operated by Little Hill Foundation, Inc., at Blairstown, New Jersey, avowedly specializes in helping the "reluctant to recover." Such people, insisted Mrs. D., need "tincture of time," "structured living," and what the "students" there often call "brainwashing." Those associated with Little Hill-Alina Lodge believe it is the only "non-permissive" alcoholism and poly-addiction rehabilitation center in the United States. It defines "non-permissiveness" as "not allowing "sympathy" to interfere with "empathy" and recovery." Although it has sometimes been perceived that the Lodge treats only the "reluctant" or "chronic relapsers" or "multiple repeaters," the program is actually available to all suffering alcoholics and their families.

Geraldine Delaney was born on June 9, 1907. She got sober on April 23, 1947, six and a half years after her brother Oscar sobered up in some of A.A.'s first years. She was a native of Illinois where she attended Knox College and the University of Illinois. She died July 9, 1998.

Recognition

From 1948 to 1963, Mrs. Delaney was Executive Director of "Chr-Ill" Services—the Essex County, New Jersey Service for the Chronically Ill. This program set a pattern for New Jersey and for the United States. A *Saturday Evening Post* article in 1955 gave an account of this Homemaker Service.

Mrs. Delaney founded the Chr-Ill Council on Alcoholism, forerunner of the New Jersey affiliate of the National Council on Alcoholism. In fact, she worked with NCA founder Marty Mann; and the New Jersey council became the first affiliate of the National Council on Alcoholism in New Jersey (As to Marty Mann and NCA, see Sally Brown and David R. Brown: *A Biography of Mrs. Marty Mann: The First Lady of Alcoholics Anonymous* MN: Hazelden, 2001). Mrs. D. served on the Governor's Advisory Council on Alcoholism in New Jersey. She has lectured at the

Rutgers School of Alcohol Studies. She served on the staff of the
Counselor Course of the Office of Economic Opportunity. And she
has lectured throughout the United States on problems of addiction
to alcohol and other "mood changers." She spoke at schools,
service organizations, churches, and professional groups. She was
honored by two Presidents of the United States (Reagan and
Clinton), by two Popes, and also by many luminaries in the field of
alcoholism.

She was awarded a plaque by The New Jersey Task Force on
Women and Alcohol as its first Annual Achievement Award
recipient. The Award states:

> For her energy and determination in the face of public
> indifference and apathy toward alcoholics
> For courage in addressing the problem of dual addiction,
> particularly in women
> For leadership in initiating quality residential treatment, not
> only for alcoholics, but for their families as well
> For administrative, organization and fund-raising abilities in
> building an institution with a national reputation
> And for her personal dedication to the physical, mental and
> spiritual recovery of the afflicted and affected

This second edition of *HOPE* contains a brief biography of the
life of Mrs. Geraldine Owen Delaney. It is also an account of her
long association with the field of alcoholism-addiction recovery, and
the philosophy of Alina Lodge, the program it uses, and the
successes it achieves.[1] We utilize Mrs. D.'s very own recollections
as well as those of her Lodge staff, alumni and alumnae, and peers.
We believe others will benefit from learning and understanding the

---

[1] For a comprehensive discussion of how professionals rate Little Hill–Alina Lodge, see
Stan Hart, *Rehab: A Comprehensive Guide to Recommended Drug-Alcohol Treatment
Centers in the United States* (New York: Harper & Row, 1988), pp. 310-15. After an
extended discussion, Hart rates the Lodge "excellent."

basic principles of the philosophy which brings hope, healing, and changed lives to many Lodge students and their families.

The stage can perhaps best be set by highlighting the motto of Little Hill-Alina Lodge: "There is a place where hope can become fact." And hope has *often* become fact at the Lodge at Blairstown, New Jersey.

Reflections

The following are some thoughts and beliefs collected by Mrs. Delaney--ideas she used in talking with others, in lectures, and in her own life:

- Alcoholics often learn their self-destructive, deceitful, and manipulative attitudes early on; and "It takes one to know one."

- Alcoholics are not necessarily alike.

- The best of the best learn somewhere along the line the vital importance of helping others.

- Alcohol is a drug. Drugs are addictive and mood-changing; and they compound the effects of each other.

- One key to helping the alcoholic is to love that person enough to tell him or her the truth and to make that person behave—something that the family is often ill-equipped to do.

- Alcoholics need to relate consequences to behavior.

- Time is vital. The new *student* alcoholic or addict requires a long time for the mind to mend enough to think clearly and direct appropriate behavior.

- Simplicity is important in the cloudy days—a by-product of which is Mrs. D.'s expression: "Don't drink. Don't drug. Go to meetings. Shut up and listen. KISS a lot (Keep it simple, stupid!).

- Structure is important.

- Discipline is important.

- Humble pie needs to be eaten and digested.

- Addiction is pain plus learned relief.

- When the trouble the bottle causes becomes greater than the peace it brings, that may be the beginning of the desire to change.

- Becoming honest about one's plight is essential to beginning a changed life.

- Change arises out of spiritual sources and forces, not from one's own knowledge or will-power or colleagues.

- One can gain faith (reliance upon the power of God) by following good, orderly direction—honesty about the problem (YOU); humility about the solution (GOD); and action to link the problem to the solution (letting go of self and letting God do what needs to be done).

- Recovery is a program which requires listening, realizing, believing, and understanding—moving the material 18 inches from head to heart.

- Recovery is returning to the good behavior that is available.

You will probably recognize most of foregoing thoughts and beliefs as you read Mrs. D.'s story in the next chapter. And now for the details.

2

Mrs. D.'s Story

[Mrs. D.'s Story is almost exactly as told on taped interviews. A minimum of editing has been done by the author.]

I was an ugly, skinny little girl with a crooked nose and a face that almost didn't come together. I was belligerent, naughty, and attention-getting. My brother was five when I was born. Mother wanted another son, but she got me. Mother wanted me to go away: Mother went away a lot.

My mother was an insecure person. She married my father–a college professor; and they went to live where his family was. He became a local banker. I saw my father drink only two times during his life. Both times he got bombed.

The first time I recall knowing anything about alcohol was a day my father and grandfather were sitting at the dining room table drinking wine. My mother said, "Don't let Geraldine see that bottle." They put it under the table. My mother was a closet drinker. She said she had a gall bladder problem. Alcohol was not available in those days, only for "medicinal purposes." Pot–they called it "weeds"–*was* available. Incidently, what they gave them for drunkenness in those days was heroin, the new drug on the market. The doctor would come over and give my mother a shot of heroin so she could go off to the church social.

13

Mother was the town dowager, and she would leave her nasty little daughter at home with the Scottish nanny who lived with us. The nanny thought I was wonderful, but she couldn't do everything. She couldn't keep track of me because I was all over like a dirty shirt.

One day, I got nasty and mother put me in a closet where she kept all her skirts. She wore ankle-length skirts, satin and velvet, with a small waist and big hips. There was a stained glass window in that closet. I got tired of watching the shadows dance through the window, and I decided to spit on every one of her skirts, systematically; and I did. When I got out of the closet, I said nothing about it. A couple of weeks later, I heard my mother say to my aunt, who lived just across the street, "Winny, we don't have any moths; but I've got white spots, about the size of my thumb nail, on every one of my skirts." Then I heard my Aunt Winny say, "Verna, have you put Geraldine in the closet recently?" And I took off. I knew my Aunt Winny knew what I'd been up to.

Because I was the daughter of one of the wealthiest men in town, I had a bicycle when most people didn't. One of my early memories is that after school, I used to ride a little girl by the name of Vivian on the handle-bars of my bicycle. Vivian lived on the "wrong side of the tracks." One day, I got mad at Vivian; and I was nasty to her, and wouldn't ride her. She never spoke to me again. I think that was the starting point of my wanting to be a help rather than a hindrance. That made me want to help people.

My mother really wanted no part of me, That's why I ran off and married a fifty-seven-year-old man when I was seventeen. That was a really quick marriage, because my mother had it annulled as soon as she found out. My husband owned the apartment building where we lived. In those days, you didn't have many apartment buildings: Apartment buildings with penthouses were very rare. My mother was so busy courting her next husband that she didn't care where I went. I was sitting in the lobby, and that is where I got mixed up with the owner, who had the penthouse. His name was Ed Young. Well she fixed that. It was a touch and go thing all the time with mamma and me and her alcoholism.

It is interesting, the differences in alcoholics. My brother was an alcoholic, and I am an alcoholic. Oscar grew up to hate my mother; and when she died, he would not even go to Florida with me to arrange for her burial. I was always in the dog house and kicked around, but I loved my mother in spite of it. My brother adored me. He was the smart one, I thought. He was five years older than I, so I didn't pay much attention to him. People keep saying to me, "You are an alcoholic because of this, that and the other thing." My brother was a "goody-two-shoes." He always did everything the teachers wanted him to do, was just adored by the teachers, and clutched by my mother. I was always in trouble with the teachers. My father was superintendent of schools, among other things, and I was always in trouble; always standing in the corner; always being punished. There was always something. Yet we had the same mother and the same father and the same upbringing. Mother was partial to my brother. That is normal for mothers and sons.

Oscar hated Mother because of her expectations of him–what he would and would not do. She set up expectations of him that were unrealistic. She never set up any expectations of me. She was so far into her alcoholism that I don't think she knew or cared much about my activities even when I became successful.

When I was eighteen, I went away to school. My self esteem was low—very low. I wanted to be popular. I found a way to be very popular. At that time, booze was outlawed in this country. I'd go to Canada and smuggle across the border two quarts of Canadian whiskey in hot water bottles strapped to my legs. I wore long cotton panties so the rubber bottles wouldn't squeak. The situation was different in those days. There wasn't the great rush—that everybody HAD to drink. I didn't start drinking when I ran booze across the border. I just wanted to be popular. With Canadian booze, I was popular.

In 1927, the beginning of the great depression, my father lost all his money. I'd never had to think about money. My father called me on the phone and told me he was broke, and I would have to make my own way. So it was, that in 1928 I went to work to support myself—seventy years ago.

When you have very low self esteem, you do anything that makes you feel better. A little before this era, medications like phenobarbital, nembutal, and seconal came on the market. At first they were available over the counter, uncontrolled. As time went on, they realized these drugs were addicting, and the government put them under control. In the meantime, I had become thoroughly addicted to mood and mind changing medications; and I liked the mood and mind changer, alcohol, the best. It was still illegal when I had my first drink.

My first job was with a group of doctors who were all writing books. They were all professors at Northwestern Medical, and I edited the various books for them. I worked for a surgeon; for an ear, nose, and throat doctor; and finally got to the pediatrician's book, which was entitled, *Babies Are Human Beings*. I asked him why he made it so simple. He looked at me like I had holes in my head, and said, "Doctors are tired at night. I want them to READ it." That was the first medical bestseller ever written. Not only the doctors read it, but also people with children read it, because it was so simple and so direct. It told them what to do.

After I had been working for some time, I hooked up with a group of doctors who had formed the first group practice in the United States. They were all specialists working together in one office. There was a standing joke among them: "We'll try the new medication on Gerry. If it doesn't kill her, it won't hurt our patients." They were laughing. I was such a nervous, jittery person. Remember, I was coming off booze every day. Strangely, that office was just around the corner from the home of one of the students in residence here now getting treatment (The year was 1991).

Eventually, we went to the Mayo Clinic in Rochester, Minnesota. Dr. Andy, a pediatrician, was invited to give a special course there on what would now be called, parenting. All we were talking about was that fathers ought to get interested in their children from the time they are conceived and all throughout their lives. They had never done anything like that before.

By this time, my drinking had gotten me in trouble many times. Yet my career seemed very successful. I was drawing a salary women never drew in those days. I had a chauffeur, an expense account, and a maid. But I kept landing in the hospital from exhaustion, and I kept fooling psychiatrists into thinking I was overworked.

I had gotten married again early in my career. You remember my first short marriage was to a man named Ed Young. This one's name was Young Love. When we were married, he had a four-year-old boy, Dick, who became my step child; and I raised him. When Dick was sixteen, his father and I were divorced. I didn't realize it at the time, but I caused the divorce. I was traveling with three doctors all over the country. When I'd come home on weekends and we'd go out, everyone would say, "Oh Gerry, where have you been this week?" They'd never ask my husband where he had been. He was a traveling trade agent, and he went the same places every week. He traveled Minnesota, Illinois, and Iowa; and he'd just make the circuit. In retrospect, I believe I literally castrated that husband, because the focus was always on me. Here I was on a handsome salary, traveling all over the country doing interesting work.

When Young Love and I were divorced, Dick came to live with me. He had been to the judge and asked to be allowed to live with me. The judge asked me if I wanted money. I said no, that I could support him. I said to Dick, "Pop was so generous. He bought you everything money could buy, and I'm so strict. Why did you want to be with me?" He didn't hesitate. He said, "Mom, you love me enough to tell the truth and make me behave." Yes, I was strict with him. I got a lot of pleasure out of that boy. He was killed in the armed forces. He had listed me as his blood mother. It almost killed his father.

I seemed to have everything, but I was dissatisfied with me. There seemed to be no consequences for what I did. I am told I drove a tractor trailer once. Yet I have no memory of it. Drinking was "perfectly normal" by my standards. Even though we know we are drinking too much, we con ourselves. We lie to ourselves more than we lie to anyone. I did almost die of an overdose in San Francisco, and I landed in the hospital for eleven days. When I got out, I just laughed it off saying, "You can't kill the Irish."

Meantime, I had this moral leper brother who drank too much. He was employed at a big job in New York, and he drank too much and was always getting in trouble. I called a psychiatrist in Newark–a child psychiatrist by the way–the only one I knew on the Eastern Seaboard. And I knew all of them. I asked him what to do with my moral leper brother. At first he said, "I don't know." Then he said, "The other night I was at a meeting, and a man by the name of Bill Wilson was talking about doing something peculiar with people who drink too much. He gave me his card. I'll call him up." And the doctor called the co-founder of Alcoholics Anonymous.[2] Bill came to see my brother Oscar and remained friend and advisor with him ever after. My brother got sober that year, 1941.

Bill was a very simple man, a very wonderful man, yet very simple. Bill became a special friend to my brother. Now, in A.A. we call this sort of friend a sponsor.

My brother did not take criticism very well. Incidentally, I don't believe any alcoholic takes criticism very well. My brother got upset because they were criticizing him for not going to enough meetings. In those early days of AA, you had to travel for miles and miles: There weren't that many meetings around. They were criticizing him, so he went to New York to talk with Bill about it. He asked Bill how many meetings he should go to. Bill sat back in his chair and said, very quietly, "Well, Oscar, how many meetings do you WANT to go to, to save your life?" That's all Bill said. You know, when we look at it, we found time to drink every day. There probably weren't meetings to go to every *day*, but there were a good many. A.A. says that any two or three people who gather together to share their experience, strength, and hope, constitute a meeting. So there could have been meetings if you wanted them. That is the way all new groups of A.A. have started.

Over the years, I went with my brother to some of these meetings. I thought it was a nice little organization for those moral lepers, like my brother, who drank too much. *I* didn't have a problem.

While at the Mayo Clinic, I began working again with Dr. Andy to form a medical organization, a national organization which became

---

[2] Bill Wilson and Dr. Bob Smith were co-founders of Alcoholics Anonymous. A.A. was born on June 10, 1935, the date Dr. Bob had his last drink.

the second national medical certifying board in the United States.[3] While we were working out there, Dr. Andy became very ill. He was dying. I just went all to pieces. Then they sent me out to Iowa to a doctor out there who was going to run the national organization for Dr. Andy. He thought he could handle me too. But I just got worse.

Over the years, it just seemed that I was fighting to not let anyone know I had a great desire for alcohol. I kept landing in hospitals and fooling psychiatrists into thinking I was overworked. It was then that I landed in the twenty-third hospital, and I convinced the twenty-third psychiatrist that I was outrageously overworked and underpaid. (I was probably one of the best paid women in the United States, and, undoubtedly, the most spoiled.)

Out of the goodness of their hearts, those doctors decided to put me on a year's leave of absence with full pay and all my side benefits. But I got incensed because they wrote me about it instead of talking to me. The arrogance of the addict had set in. I told them what they could do with their job, and they did it. They gave me a five-figure bonus, and I went on a tear. I got drunk all over the country. I have no idea where I went, or what I was doing, or where the money went.

One morning, I found myself in a psychiatric lock-up ward on the West Side of Chicago, with iron bars on the windows, an iron bed, my clothes draped over an iron chair, no doorknobs, and a peep hole in the door. SUDDENLY, I HAD A BIG PROBLEM.

It took me twenty years to tell anybody how I'd gotten there. It seems that I was in a nightclub with a group of doctors, and decided to do a striptease act while I was drinking. They didn't think that would look good in the newspapers, so they locked me up.

I promised myself, "If I ever get out of here, I will ask my brother to help me." My brother had been called several times before, once from San Francisco when I had been so sick from an overdose. He had never come. But this time he knew it was the time. He borrowed money from his friends and came to Chicago to see me. He said to me very simply, "Honey, you've made a pretty lousy mess of your life.

---

[3] Mrs. D. frequently refers to her twenty years of experience in pediatrics, and her association with the certification group is a major reason for her reference.

Do you want to do something about it?" Well, I did: But I didn't want to go with that bunch of holy rollers (AAs) who were praying all the time. Like all alcoholics, I was a liar.

I have since come up with a simple definition of the alcoholic that suits me without going into a lot of gobbledygook. I believe that anyone who allows alcohol or the alcohol-like drugs to interfere with his or her life in any way, and doesn't bring it to a screeching halt, is an alcoholic. If drinkers continue on, trying to hit the bottle, it is because they don't want to give up the one thing that has given them emotional peace, although temporary. And the peace they got from the bottle was better than the trouble. It is when the trouble becomes paramount that they begin to want to change. I was in big trouble. I began to want to do something; not what everybody else was doing, but *something*.

People say that it was probably those doctors overworking me that caused my drinking. No, it wasn't. You drink for one reason, and one reason only. You drink because you like what it does to you.

When my brother had come to take me from the Chicago lock-up, he had asked if I wanted to do something about my drinking. I had answered "Yes." But my fingers were crossed. He took me East and suggested how I might begin. I refused. So he left me in the lobby of a hotel without any money. I thought I was dying. I went to the ladies room and shook and shivered. When I came out, my brother took me into his home in Maplewood. He and his wife never left me alone. They took me to [A.A.] meetings. I would say, "I don't feel like going." "Who asked you if you wanted to go to a meeting? You drank every night, didn't you?" would be his answer. "I'm not dressed," I'd whine. He would answer, "Then I'll dress you." "Never mind, I'll dress myself," I'd say. Every night, my brother and his wife took me to a meeting, and it always seemed like three meetings. There was always a car full having a meeting on the way to one, then there was the meeting, and another meeting in the car coming home. Dr. Harold Murray became my mentor. My brother knew never to answer my questions. Those nearest and dearest don't know *anything*. I got smart. I got cocky. And I got sober. I could eat but was awfully, awfully sick.

When I had been sober eight months, I'd had enough of A.A. I wasn't a REAL alcoholic, and I decided to go back to Chicago and join my friends and drink like a lady. I never wanted to be anything but a lady anyhow. I was working at St. Michael's at the time, and I decided that I would take some of the money I had saved and buy a ticket to Chicago. I didn't tell anybody about my plans. Then I packed my suitcases and stuffed them back under the bed. I knew my sister-in-law wouldn't find them because I wouldn't let her in my room. I was living in *her* house, you understand, but I was a bitch.

Bill Wilson, my brother's friend, had given me a copy of the A.A. *Big Book*, the original edition, when he came to the house. I thought it was a terribly written book, and I threw it out the window into a snow bank. It reappeared on the night table. I threw it in with the dirty clothes thinking it would go to the laundry. It came back on the night table. I threw it into the garbage. Back it came, a little juicy and stained.

That was the night I packed my bags. The next morning, I would walk out on my brother. His wife didn't want me there to begin with, (and rightly so, though I couldn't see her reason at the time). I could escape in the morning after my brother had gone to work, while my sister-in-law was driving the kids to school. That evening we went to the AA meeting at South Orange.

I don't know what I heard.

But I came home that night, and there was that book that had legs there on the night table.[4] I picked it up, and it fell open to page 70, the chapter "How it Works" in the old edition. And, for the beginning of what I call a "spiritual experience," I started to read it. That word HONEST in the first paragraph was about two inches high. Then, I read down through the twelve steps. I didn't realize it until later, but I read them in the first person. I found out later that Bill had actually written them in the first person to begin with. He had some ideas, and the boys had told him to put them down in writing. It was a few of the early A.A. people who were part of the Oxford Group who were

---

[4] The references to "that book" are to *Alcoholics Anonymous*, the basic text of A.A., and to the First Edition which was published in the Spring of 1939.

putting the book together. After they got through working it over, the language was changed from "I" to "We."[5] I read the steps in the first person, read one paragraph more, closed the book, and went to sleep–still intending to sneak out, being a phony. The next morning, I awakened, sat up on the edge of the bed, and suddenly realized I'd had the first decent night's sleep I'd had since I got sober. You see, I had taken a lot of drugs, and I didn't sleep well (It takes a long while for chemicals to leave your body). Sitting there, one more realization: The desire to leave had left me–never to return–from that day to this. The desire to leave and the desire to drink–gone. That, to me, had to come from a power outside myself which I had nothing to do with. That is MY spiritual experience. It [the desire to leave or escape, and to drink and use] lifted, and has never returned. I have never again wanted to run away, or to drink, or take drugs. It was that morning I first admitted that I was an alcoholic. This experience was probably as influential as anything has been to me in my life. My growth began. I began to go to A.A., not critical, not to observe, but for *me*.

In the early days of A.A., the *family* went to all the sessions. If you had a special problem, you got together after with a couple of friends. You might go to someone's house or to a coffee shop. The spouses would sit in one booth and the alcoholics in another. There were almost no women alcoholics in A.A. at that time [Mrs. D. added: Although there weren't women in A.A. in those early days, there were and there are many women alcoholics. But they would let them die at home in their bedrooms. These are the women we hear of in history who "went to bed . . . and died"]. The women were very good to me: They let me sit with them. For this I will be forever grateful.

Yet I was always wanting to talk at meetings. Every time I got talking, the boys would say, "Shut up." They didn't want girls in that nice little men's organization, and they made it quite clear. I said to a

---

[5] The "multi-lith" copy of the Big Book was circulated before publication of the First Edition. It did not contain the word "we." However, it did not contain the word "I." A.A. itself claims that the original manuscript no longer exists; so it is not possible to learn whether this statement is correct.

little sawed off sergeant from Fort Monmouth who was chairman at the South Orange group, "I thought you could do A.A. any way you wanted to." He looked down his nose at me, the little squirt, and said, "You don't *have* a way." They were sober. They had found a way. Was it their way? No. It was the way of the winners. I couldn't see it yet. This incident was probably the second most influential factor in my recovery.

I found it very hard in the beginning. I just couldn't seem to get it through my thick head that you had to *listen*. Through my brother, I was exposed to the wisdom of Bill Wilson and his wife, Lois [Mrs. D. added: In 1951, out of sheer necessity, Lois Wilson founded Al-Anon, which soon came to include Alateen].[6]

In his simple way, Bill urged, "Don't drink, don't drug, go to meetings, and shut up." They didn't want women, but they let me sit there. I had to listen; I had to learn; I had to act, and feel, and believe before I could "pass it on."

Early on, I had to tell those A.A. folks that I didn't believe in God. Instead of having a fit about it, they calmly said, "How about Good Orderly Direction. Can you believe in that?" I found that just fine. The God of my understanding gives me good orderly direction still. I was slow letting go. I was slow believing. I was slow accepting. I did not want to let go and let "Good Orderly Direction," or GOD, as I understand Him now, do what needs to be done.

Even when I had that spiritual experience, I did not recognize it as such. It wasn't until I began to grow that I came to realize what had happened: A power greater than I was had brought me a moment of feeling–a moment of sanity that kept me from killing myself. "Why didn't I go back to Chicago that morning in 1947?" I wondered later. I couldn't. Why couldn't I go? God wouldn't let me. I would have been dead. But I didn't know that yet.

---

[6] Although Al-Anon ideas were germinated before 1951 in Akron and on the East Coast, Al-Anon, said Lois Wilson in her memoirs, "did not take its own shape until 1951." Officially, Al-Anon was said to be founded by Lois Wilson and Anne B. The two women were called "Co-Founders."

We see ourselves after the fact, through other people; and this is the primary reason for going to A.A. meetings. We don't know what day we are going to see and hear what we need the most. You might say, "I don't get anything out of some meetings." The fact that you don't get ANYTHING out of it makes one wonder how you are thinking. Are you thinking negatively? Certainly not positively. It was the little things, as I went along, that I came to realize; came to believe; came to understand; came to listen for. We came to it slowly. We say, "I heard you," but it never went farther than the front of our face. The distance from your head to your heart is eighteen inches. As my grandfather used to say, "That's a FUR piece."

There was a clubhouse in Newark which my brother Oscar had helped get started. A year after I got sober, I was down there one evening. I overheard two men talking. "That sister of his might be a nice girl, but she's got a screw loose." It was me they were talking about.

Shortly after that, I fell in love with an Irishman, Thomas Frances D. He had come into the program about the same time I did. He was sober, and I was sober. We were going to meetings all over everyplace. I loved him, and I married him. Was my life serene now? NO. It is awfully difficult to marry another alcoholic. Men and women are NOT alike. In order to live together, each needs to use the very best of what is in the person. I didn't know that then. I was in love, and I began to cherish EVERYTHING.

I wanted to get well faster than I was getting well; and when I was sober three years, I went to see the great Dr. Ruth Fox, the psychiatrist who brought Antabuse to this country. I said, "Ruth, I'm just not progressing as fast as I should." She asked, "How long have you been sober?" "Three years," I answered. She looked at me a few minutes and said, "Gerry, it takes two years to get your brains out of hock, and three more to get them unscrambled, and *then* you begin to grow." I thought she'd just flipped out. She was right. It takes a long time for you to *really* get into the program. This was probably the third most influential experience in my recovery.

I was sober six or seven months before I started to work, and was able to become productive again. I think I always wanted to help people. Because I had worked in the field of pediatrics for twenty years, I knew influential doctors in this area of New Jersey. They helped me get started. I began to do projects that were helpful to people–information centers, services that people, sick over long periods of time, needed. I formed what was known as *Essex County Services for the Chronically Ill*. I knew there were women in the community who could help out people who were sick. The women could work for a few hours a day, and they might like to make a little money. My brother was teaching at Rutgers at the time. He got some people from Rutgers to come up and talk with these women and establish a formal course. That is how we started teaching homemakers some of the things they needed to know. They were able to help the chronically ill. That is how the service got its name Chr-Ill (pronounced "Krill"). This was the first homemaker service in New Jersey. It became the pattern for others, not only in New Jersey, but also throughout the nation. My first project was what is now known as "a homemaker-home health aide service."

Another project was to set up what we called then, the Committee on Alcoholism. Marty Mann was beginning her work forming the National Council on Alcoholism, and she used to come out here to the Lodge and spend the weekend. National Council does not have any affiliation with Alcoholics Anonymous. You see, Bill Wilson wanted to help Marty Mann with the National Council. The AA boys objected to it. They objected to his using his name William Wilson. So he decided to help her on the side. He provided her with a lot of help. In New Jersey, we already had this Committee on Alcoholism, organized under the Essex County Service for the Chronically Ill. That New Jersey committee became the second branch of the National Council. However, Marty Mann wanted the recognition that alcoholism is a medical affair, and the committee had to come under the medical society. It was in that era that alcoholism was beginning to be recognized nationally as a chronic disease.[7]

---

[7] Today the organization founded by Marty Mann has its headquarters in New York and is known as the National Council on Alcoholism and Drug Dependence.

It was during this time, while going to A.A., that I met a German girl about my age. Her name was Ina Trevis. During the rise of Nazism in Germany, Ina (Elina Rudolph Trevis) had been working to help Jewish people escape. Ina had two brothers, one a physician, whom she thought was a Nazi sympathizer though he actually was not. She would steal his passport, give it to a Jewish person, and ferry the refugee across the border to safety. Then she would walk back across the border, drunk, and flirt with the guards, thereby helping people escape Nazi Germany. During this time, she met and married a Dutch artist, Newmark Trevis, who became Curator of the Huntington Art Museum in California where he had taken his wife in order to get away from the Nazis. But living in California did not work as far as Ina's alcoholism was concerned.

Back in New York, Ina awoke one morning, having been drunk the night before. She found her husband dead from a heart attack. Ina went to High Watch Farm in Kent, Connecticut. In those days, High Watch was not a rehabilitation site for alcoholics as it is today, but a religious retreat supported by a woman who, I believe, was English. People spent the winter up there on the mountain with outside water, outside toilets, and nothing but a stove for heat. Ina got sober there.[8]

---

[8] The High Watch Farm brochure states in part: High Watch Farm is a residential facility for admitted alcoholic dependent men and women. It functions as a quiet retreat rather than a hospital or treatment center. It was established in 1939. . . . High Watch adheres to a simple philosophy:—that a spiritual conversion, by the application of the twelve suggested steps of Alcoholics Anonymous to daily life, can take place. . . . At High Watch, we have seven [A.A.] meetings each week, five afternoon and two evening meetings. These meetings include step meetings, discussion meetings and "Big Book" meetings. . . . There are daily chapel services, non religious in content or intent; they are expressions of experience, hope, and insight into the process of recovery. [High Watch is located] on the "Hill of Hope." There is a croquet court, horse shoes and basketball hoop. Television is available. . . as well as VCR for movies and tapes. Tables are there for cards and other games. . . . High Watch Farm is the oldest residential facility in the world which employs the principles of Alcoholics Anonymous as its only therapy. . . . The Farm's former owner, Etheldred Folsom, known as "Sister Francis" was introduced to the A.A. program by its co-founder Bill Wilson and Marty Mann. So impressed by their program and their efforts, "Sister Francis" asked Bill Wilson if he would like to take over the Farm as a retreat for those who needed the quiet setting and the work in order to begin their recovery. In 1940 a Board of Directors was appointed so that this generous gift could be accepted and still remain within the Twelve
(continued...)

It was about this time we [Ina and Gerry] met each other through AA. Ina loved alcoholics, and she wanted to help them. There was a place on Route 46 in Parsippany called Ailanthus Hall. It was an old baronial castle. Connie and Emily Hanson had rented the old place, and they were trying to sober up some sick alcoholics. There were only 6 or 7 people there, but they wanted someone to cook. Ina applied for the job, and got it. She couldn't cook. So she bought a cook book. They stayed open only six or seven months after she got there (I used to go out there with Susan B. Anthony). When that place closed, a lawyer named Al helped Ina rent a house in Kenville. She started a lodge there which took in alcoholics. That's where our name "Alina" originated.

It took some time for the medical world to accept the fact that alcoholism is a medical affair. In 1956, the American Medical Association declared alcoholism a chronic disease. Ina thought that this would mean that alcoholics would go to the hospital for treatment. Her dream became the establishment of a retreat where recovering alcoholics might come to vacation untempted by alcohol. She found this tract of land, 100 acres on the Paulinskill River, an old apple farm with a stone house on it. The area that Ina found was known as Little Hill. She was determined to buy that land.

Ina called me at my office in Essex County and said she couldn't obtain mortgage financing for two weeks and was going to lose that land. Could I lend her the money? I said, "Ina, I don't have that kind of money." "Yes," she said, "but you have credit because you've got a job, and you've got a husband." Finally I gave in, borrowed the money, and loaned it to her on unsecured notes. She bought the farm. The mortgage did not come through in two weeks, nor in four weeks. Six weeks later, Ina dropped dead of a heart attack, and I was left with unsecured notes.

---

[8](...continued)
Traditions of A.A. High Watch Farm was established as a non-profit corporation. It has not been involved in insurance payments. . . [This material has been included because of similarities between High Watch and the Lodge and also because of the origins of the Lodge itself].

So we started this lodge against my will. I did *not* want to work in the field of alcohol rehabilitation. I enjoyed the work I was doing. So I stayed with my Essex County job and thought I could set this place up in a few months. That was 1957. It was obvious, however, that Little Hill was not going to be a vacation spot. People were sick, and there was no place for them to go.

We became Little Hill Foundation for the Rehabilitation of Alcoholics, Inc. The property had a carriage house and the old stone house with a little wood house attached, which we later turned into bedrooms. There were no driveways, no sidewalks, just apple trees. The people around the area did not object because we agreed to pay taxes. Of course we sometimes wish we hadn't agreed to pay taxes as they are high on our many acres. But the amount of good will generated by those taxes is probably worth the money. The people have not objected, have been interested, not nosey, but cooperative and supportive.

Although Ina and I had vacationed together in Sanibel, Florida, a few times, I had no idea she had a heart problem. I knew very little about her family other than the fact she had two brothers. After she died, those brothers surfaced. They wanted money. I didn't have it to give them. I believe fate played a great part here. I had a Jewish lawyer who happened to have sold the most UJA Bonds, and he won a trip to Europe. Guess where he wanted to go? He wanted to visit a little town in Germany where his grandfather had been born. Guess who lived in this same town? Yes, the brothers of Ina. They settled the argument.

Ina died just before Christmas time. She loved Christmas. We tried to make it her usual Christmas—trying to go on with all the things she loved, decorations everywhere, the little German figures. We hadn't gotten around to organized carol singing. But faintly in the distance we heard singing, starting from the old carriage house, just a few voices singing Christmas carols. One was that of a Jewish fellow singing carols. (His son became a student here too and is doing well, lives on the West Coast.)

By 1963, I gave up my Essex County job, and we moved here. I ran the Lodge over thirty-five years. Even now, Christmas is very special. We do a lot of decorating, have our own traditions, candles, and much singing. And we remember Ina.

We are now the most successful long-term place in the country. We are geared to help all alcoholics, including the "Reluctant to Recover." The fact is that most alcoholics *can* recover *if* they are *willing* to do the work, and not just look for a "magic cure."

What we use at the lodge is *Tincture of Time*; that is, time away, structured living, three meals, regular hours. It takes "Tincture of Time" to rid your system of a combination of chemicals that have been stored there over the years. The other thing that helps the "reluctant to recover" is what our students call "brainwashing." My comment on this, in usual "Grambo" fashion, is: "What is *in* your brain isn't any good. So let's get on with the washing, and put in the positive material that will make you live."

It has been many years that a lot of people have been working as hard as we could, hoping to God something would happen. (Some breakthrough in the treatment of alcoholism.) We are still hoping. The problems here [in the field of treatment] are far from solved, *FAR* from solved.

You know, some people in A.A. don't like you to talk about drugs. Yet alcohol is the oldest known drug of addiction, and it IS A DRUG. As Doctor Gitlow used to say, "Drugs are nothing but dehydrated alcohol in different strengths."[9]

Whether the drugs are liquid or solid or smoked, makes not one whit of difference. The thing is that we cannot keep people away from alcohol if they are going to take other mood and mind changers. They return to the drug of choice, which is alcohol. The only known cure for alcoholism is abstinence. Many times alcohol smells. So they change to pills during the day and drink at night. The first thing you know, you have three or four chemicals in the system at the same time, and one plus one doesn't equal two when it's chemicals. It makes a compound which is much stronger.

---

[9] Stanley E. Gitlow, M.D., is Clinical Professor of Medicine, Mt. Sinai School of Medicine.

I still regret that they didn't name addiction "Jellinek's disease" after the great Doctor Jellinek who did so much for alcoholism addiction.[10] It would be easy to blanket all these things. Though the program was originally designed for alcohol, it works just great with all addictions. Remember, addiction is pain plus learned relief.

We have got a problem here that is FAR from solved. A.A. is overrun with people now. In the early days, there were ten sober alcoholics to one new one. Now, to every twenty new ones there is one sober one. So the newcomer doesn't get the one-on-one attention. They don't get the things they need. Outpatient therapy is trying to help with this, but it doesn't have the same charisma that the A.A. fellowship has for the alcoholic. Nor do they tend to talk about spirituality in outpatient therapy. I believe one of the GREATEST things about A.A. is its urge that you believe in a power greater than yourself.

There is much, much more to do in the field of alcoholism. We are going through a very hard time now, because insurance companies have shut down on their payments. And it is the fault of the profit seekers, private enterprise.

Many years ago, Marty Mann and some of the rest of us went down to Washington to talk with them about the insurance companies covering the alcoholic, after alcoholism was declared a chronic disease. We said that we would work to cut down on the "revolving door." That is when all these many new programs stepped in. The programs have made the revolving door *worse*. The insurance companies have now shut down. They won't pay. They're paying some–for a few of them, particularly companies that have big contracts. One girl came in here for long term. Incidently, she is sober now, and she is doing advertising for a rather famous company. This little girl came in here after twenty-eight days in a New Jersey establishment (which will remain nameless). The bill for her twenty-eight days in *that* place was $38,000.00. That sort of thing has turned the insurance companies off. Now, programs are trying to turn them

---

[10] E. M. Jellinek delineated the disease concept of alcoholism.

back on, but they're having a hell of a time with it. We are far from a position of saying we've got alcohol under control. We do not.

There are still a lot of people who do not accept the fact that alcohol IS A DRUG. They think alcohol is all right. Some of them have people right in their own family who are alcoholic. When I ask them to stop, some of them do, and some of them say no. Some do stop. I talked to one father recently whose son is in the Lodge recovering. The father stopped drinking for one hundred three days. Then he started drinking again. You know what I think? I think we'll get him in here.

Everything good in my life has happened because I am sober. The greatest miracle for me is that the desire to run away went away. That was the beginning of my life. I have been asked to do things I do not want to do. Doing them has brought a little peace of mind and soul. I have these because of what A.A. brings to me. It would be O.K. with me if the God of my understanding were to call me tonight. The buildings at Alina Lodge have been built with gratitude money. We get the cash first, and then we build. A.A. gives me faith: If it is right, it will come to pass. I know serenity. For me, serenity is freedom from the mini storms. Something minor is always bugging us. I can change *me*. Serenity requires courage; courage to change things in my life that need changing: Changing bad thinking to good habits. Bad thinking leads to drinking. We *earn* the right to have our own opinion.

There is an unhappy part of my life. My husband Tom and I had been married twenty years, and we lived here in Blairstown. Tom was a contractor, and he had a bad back. Sober twenty-two years, Tom was active in A.A. While away, a friend of his offered him muscle relaxants, and the two agreed, "Don't tell Gerry." They knew how I feel about drugs. "I have never seen a druggie who doesn't drink and vice versa." The muscle relaxants helped Tom's back. He also had a cough. So his friend gave him a non-alcoholic cough medicine. It contained triple bromide. Tom took it. Two days later, he was in the bar drinking. He was hospitalized fourteen times in seventeen months. Tom had been sober three weeks the day he died. I vowed the day he died that I will not stop talking about drugs *and* alcohol.

My brother, Oscar, would have been sober fifty-two years this November, and well over ninety. He and his wife, and Lois and Bill Wilson were my closest friends, and they are all dead. And of course my dear husband Tom is dead. So many people speak of him with respect and love. That is the reason I didn't go to the last International A.A. Convention in Seattle in 1990. I just couldn't face it.

A.A. has saved my life, and my sanity, and has allowed me to help others. How often do you need to go to meetings? How many meetings do you want to go to save your life? A.A. is a way of life. Don't be ashamed of your disease. Realize you are the strongest of the strong.

That's my story. May I just add a few ideas I find useful? They are not original. When I find an idea I like, I borrow it and pull it out to use when I need it. Here are some:

- There are very few things in life we can change. There are many things about which we can change our attitude.

- The secret of happy living is not to do what you like, but to like what you do.

- If you think you can do something, you are probably right. If you think you cannot do something, you are probably right also.

- The greatness of a person is not evidenced by finding faults, but by fixing them.

- In every trouble there is a blessing.

- Out of suffering come the strongest souls: God's wounded often make his best soldiers.

- The really happy person is the one who can enjoy the scenery even when it is necessary to take a detour.

- Hate is a prolonged manner of emotional and spiritual suicide.

3

The Lodge: A Place of Hope Become Fact

Many of the earliest, best, and most long-lived recoveries in early A.A. began in private homes–usually following brief hospitalization for detoxification. Dr. Bob's home in Akron sheltered many A.A. pioneers who stayed for months, recovered, and then went on to carry their message of hope.

There were other homes in Akron, Ohio, which produced similar results—the homes of Tom L. and Wally G. and their respective wives, for example. Early AAs recognized quite soon that alcoholics in the initial stages of withdrawal often required sheltered care. But what some called "baby-sitting" in private homes became both impractical and potentially dangerous as time went on. The demands on the families of Dr. Bob and Anne Smith, Bill and Lois Wilson, Tom L., Wally G. and others were very burdensome. Some perceived a need for centers to care for the acutely ill alcoholic and provide extended care and rehabilitation.

Ina Rudolph Trevis was one who early recognized this need. Ina, a German actress, had moved to Holland with her Dutch husband prior to the outbreak of World War II. She believed her physician brother to be a Nazi sympathizer; and she stole his identification papers. With these and her own papers, she began spiriting many German scientists and professionals out of Nazi Germany and across the border to safety. She became a member of the German underground. Time and again, she risked her life in this endeavor as she became the flirting drunk to disarm and divert the attention of border guards. Then, she strongly suspected that her own brothers were Nazis who would soon turn her in; and she and her husband fled. She took her belongings *and her disease of alcoholism* with her.

Eventually, Ina and her husband arrived in the United States. Her husband became curator of a museum on the West Coast of the United States. By this time, however, Ina had become a *real* alcoholic. Her husband and her friends (many of the same psychiatrists, psychologists, and M.D.'s she had formerly helped to freedom) tried to help Ina with her drinking problem. Then Ina's husband died; and Ina's alcoholism progressed rapidly. Not until she joined Alcoholics Anonymous did she gain sobriety. She did, however, gain a strong conviction that she had to help sick alcoholics who wanted sobriety.

Ina became acquainted with an English nurse who owned land in Kent, Connecticut. Sister Frances, as this nurse was called, wished to have her property used for spiritual purposes. Ina and her friends urged Sister Frances to utilize her land to help alcoholics because they believed that only by spiritual means do alcoholics achieve recovery. The land in Connecticut became High Watch Farm, the first non-profit "farm" for alcoholics. Ina spent many months at High Watch; and though there was a very hard winter without heat and indoor plumbing, this seemed only to strengthen Ina's resolve to dedicate the rest of her life to helping alcoholics recover.

Ina left High Watch and came to New Jersey. There she secured a job as a cook at Ailanthus Hall in 37 Parsippany. Ailanthus was a small residential home run by Connie and Emily Hanson for the purpose of detoxifying alcoholics. Ina applied for the job of cook though she did not know how to boil water. Eight years later, Connie and Emily moved to Vermont; and Ina determined to establish a place of her own. She felt there should be more facilities similar to those at High Watch and Ailanthus Hall. Ina had a friend who was a lawyer named Al Silverman, whom she had persuaded to her cause.

Al Silverman and Ina Trevis established a facility in Kenvil, New Jersey. Al and Ina called the place Alina Lodge (combining the Al and the Ina to form the first part of the Lodge's name). Alina Lodge existed at Kenvil for eight years; and those were difficult years with sparse help and little money. However Ina did help many alcoholics to find the road to recovery.

In the mid 1950's, professional health agencies and organizations such as the World Health Organization and the America Medical Association began to describe alcoholism as a medical disease (See E. M. Jellinek, *The Disease Concept of Alcoholism*. CT: College and University Press, 1960). A hospital in New Jersey reserved several beds for "detox." And Ina Trevis believed that all *hospitals* would provide this service and that the service would be paid for by patient insurance. She concluded her efforts would not be required in that realm.

She therefore turned her thoughts to starting a retreat-like center similar to High Watch Farm. There were small farms up for sale in Sussex and Warren County, New Jersey, and Ina began looking for a new location. She found a piece of property, consisting of more than eighty acres, and known as Little Hill, in Hardwick Township outside of Blairstown, New Jersey. The property was a non-working farm with a house that had been built in the Pre-Revolutionary War Period and used during the Civil War as a part of the underground railroad for the slaves coming north. There was, however, a major problem. Ina did not have the financial resources to buy it.

Ina had made several good friends through Ailanthus and Alcoholics Anonymous. These included Tom and Geraldine Delaney. Ina had been assured she could obtain a mortgage quickly. On that supposition, Mr. and Mrs. Tom Delaney advanced $50,000.00 of their own money to close the deal at Little Hill. They took unsecured notes and were promised they would be paid back in full as soon as the mortgage loan came through. The purchase was consummated. The *second* Alina Lodge opened in August of 1959, but it had a new name: Little Hill-Alina Lodge. However, Ina had miscalculated the anticipated entry of hospitals into the treatment field; and her clientele remained much as they had been at the *first* Alina Lodge.

When Little Hill-Alina Lodge opened, it handled four or five people in residence at any given time. These would stay for a week or so and return home. Unknown to even her closest friends, however, Ina had a serious heart condition for which digitalis had been prescribed. Ina had felt if people knew of her condition, they would not assist her in her project. The mechanics of the project involved the proposed formation of a non-profit corporation with a board of trustees. Ina was to run the facility; and the trustees were to raise and help with money, incentive, advice, and volunteer work. Ina then expressed a desire to will the property to a non-profit foundation; and her will was drawn to effectuate the plan.

Ina's will was to be signed the morning of December 11, 1959; but that was a short day with long consequences. Ina did not appear for the signing of the will. She was found dead of a heart attack on the second floor of the historic Stone House at Alina. And it was left to a small band of her friends to deal with Ina's dream.

On December 18, 1959, Little Hill Foundation for the Rehabilitation of Alcoholics, Inc. was incorporated in the State of Delaware. The foundation began with a board of five trustees which included Tom and Geraldine Delaney. The board decided to continue with the project at Little Hill-Alina Lodge to protect the personal investments. A snag was encountered almost immediately. The mortgage loan did not come through. Ina's relatives in Germany were recalcitrant, and Ina had died intestate, which meant that her relatives would receive the lodge property. However, one of the trustees had won a trip to Germany for selling the most United Jewish Appeal Bonds. His travel plans included visiting the very town where Ina's heirs lived. The board member took the necessary papers with him to Germany; and he obtained from Ina's heirs a relinquishment of the property to the newly organized Little Hill Foundation.

Mrs. Geraldine Owen Delaney became the first Executive Director and Founder of the Foundation. At that time, she was still serving full-time as Executive Director of CHR-ILL. And she spent four years wearing the two hats and guiding the destiny of Little Hill-Alina Lodge. Often, she was required the make the four-hour round-trip from her CHR-ILL office to the Lodge. Then, in 1963, she gave up the CHR-ILL post and took up full-time residence at the Lodge—with her husband, Tom Delaney, assisting her with the project.

When she began her full-time post at the Little Hill premises, Mrs. D. soon learned that the five to twelve people in residence were doing very little with the time they were spending at the Lodge. Mrs. D. had been trained by a renowned pediatrician; and because of that training, she believed that consistent discipline was required for sound learning to take place. She regularly commented: "Every decision has consequences—some good and some bad. You must be prepared to accept those consequences." She also believed that *self*-discipline had to be acquired if her late-stage alcoholic residents were to have any real chance of recovering. From these two ideas came the trademark of Little Hill-Alina Lodge: The Non-permissive Approach! And this was followed by the widespread statement in the professional and A.A. community that: When all else has failed in the effort to help someone get sober, "Send them to Gerry D. at the Lodge."

1964 marked the year when Tom Delaney, male residents at the Lodge, and local craftsmen renovated the barn. Previously, a carriage house on the premises had been renovated. And these two projects increased the bed capacity from 12 to 30 residents. Initially these residents were called "patients;" for this assured compliance with the Lodge's license as a home for sheltered care. Yet the Lodge was not established for such a purpose; and the license was dropped. A statute on the New Jersey books stipulated that unless a facility had bed-patients, the term "patient" was not to be used. Residents therefore became known as "resident guests," in keeping with the High Watch Farm tradition.

To Geraldine Delaney, however, this "resident guest" moniker smacked of someone's "privileged atmosphere" with people arriving with golf clubs and the like. She often said: "I didn't send out invitations!" In the mid-sixties, the Little Hill trustees agreed with Mrs. D. that the "residents" were present on the premises to *learn* about their disease and to *relearn* how to live successfully—free of mood-and-mind-altering chemicals. Hence the name "**student**" was coined for the residents. They were to understand clearly that they were in treatment to *learn*; and an educational model was adopted.

Gradually, Mrs. Delaney and the trustees learned that "**time**" was an essential component in the treatment of the poly-addicted alcoholic (an alcoholic who uses more than one mood or mind-changing chemical). *Time* was also essential for those who were "reluctant to recover" (the "hard to sell"). Dr. Paul Fagan—long-time board member and friend of the alcoholic—prescribed the formula for recovery at the Lodge: "**Tincture of Time!**"

At first, there was a required stay of four weeks. However, it became apparent that each student was different, and set time requirements were impossible. Factors which warrant consideration--such as age, sickness of the student upon entrance, professional and other life experiences, prior awareness and treatment--all have had a bearing upon the students' length of stay. But progress at the Lodge was not without its difficulties of all kinds. In the mid-sixties, a tragedy occurred. Geraldine's husband Tom strained his back. A well-meaning friend suggested that Tom try a muscle relaxant. Tom had never been a pill taker, and he vowed not to tell his wife Gerry that he was using the relaxant because, as he said, "She's a nut on those things." Tom, however, was unaware of the trigger effect the pills would produce. In a few weeks, the same friend suggested that Tom take some non-alcoholic cough medicine for a cough. But the medicine contained bromides which were dangerous for the alcoholic.

In the next seventeen months, Tom—a "real" alcoholic—was in fourteen hospitals. Finally, he bled to death of an esophageal hemorrhage. During this same period, Tom appeared on the Lodge premises intoxicated and held his wife Gerry at gun-point for twenty minutes. And the entire episode convinced Mrs. D. she should never stop warning alcoholics about the **dangers of other drugs**. The brain, she said, is a chemical reactor and reacts to such chemicals whenever they are present—regardless of "why" or "how" they get into the alcoholic's system. This reaction, she believed, often triggers the alcoholic's compulsive mechanism and too often with fatal consequences.

The Lodge grew; and more and more "situations" arose. Guidelines were expanded to prevent such situations from jeopardizing a student's recovery.

A "**buddy system**" was established. A student with some recovery under his or her belt was assigned to a new student for the first two weeks. The purpose was in part instructional and in part supervisory. Both the old and the new student were believed to benefit from the experience.

Then a "**non-fraternization**" policy was adopted to prevent students from becoming emotionally involved with the opposite sex. Some AAs., from the Fellowship's early days, had often suggested that "men stick with men, and women stick with women." And prior to the non-fraternization policy at the Lodge, tragic circumstances had occurred involving those who had entered "relationships" before they had the judgment to handle them. The result had sometimes been relapse and death.

Diversion from Alina program activities was severely limited. The alcoholic, it was believed, seems to look at everything but self, at all costs. Television hours were restricted in the evening. Magazines and novels, as well as professional journals, were prohibited. Visiting was restricted to one day a week; and ultimately "visiting day" became "education day." Student relatives were at the Lodge, they were told, primarily for education and not for visitation.

In the early 70's, two events of major significance occurred.

The first was the **opening of Gratitude Hall**. This was a vision of Mrs. D.'s. She felt there should be an **educational center** at the Lodge. Existing structures were being used to the maximum, and more space was needed. Gratitude Hall fulfilled the vision. It provided a **combination dining room, living quarters, lecture room, and large room for A.A. meetings and other gatherings**.

The second event involved Mrs. D.'s **vision of a structured program for the family which would include a residential feature**. She gave a task to a young trustee whose mother had been a student at the Lodge in the Sixties. (In keeping with our policy of anonymity, we shall call him Michael). Michael was to explore other programs and advise Mrs. Delaney what should be done at the Lodge. He found little was being done in the area of family therapy. He proposed some ideas for Mrs. D. to review, and she agreed with his proposals. She invited Michael to implement them; and in 1973, the Family Program at Alina Lodge was established. By 1974, **Family Hall was opened** on the premises. It was the **first residential building in the United States established for the treatment of *relatives* of alcoholics.**

The two events increased the student bed capacity to sixty and facilitated treating alcoholism as a Family Disease.

Mrs. D. was insistent upon dignity for the suffering and recovering alcoholic. Quarters were clean and comfortable. A student work therapy program helped students regain a sense of responsibility to the community. More renovations and new structures occurred with the aim of assisting recovery needs. In 1973, a wing of bedrooms was added to "The Roost." In the mid-seventies, "the Barn" (Thomas Delaney Hall) was renovated; and the "White House" (Rudolph Hall), which had been covered with stucco, was sand-blasted to reveal the original field stone structure beneath. Two new residential wings were added to the stone house in 1978. Then, in 1980, Hope Hall, a residence hall for women, was completed.

Couples' Groups began in the late 1970's as part of the Family Program. These groups provided vital aftercare for couples having difficulty adjusting to early sobriety. The Family Program itself was expanded in 1983 to offer a residential week on a scholarship basis to relatives of alcoholics who did not have someone in treatment at the Lodge. **Groups were set up for parents, spouses, and adult children of alcoholics. The program became known as the Noble Experience and was offered free of charge**.

A strong alumni body began to take shape as alumni groups and organizations formed throughout the United States. These groups provided contacts for newly discharged students, "buddies" for student relatives, and structured discussion meetings in which former students could reinforce teachings they had received at the Lodge. The alumni groups aided fund-raising for the "self-help fund." Monthly luncheons provided outreach to the recovering community, as well as former students, their relatives, and Noble Experience participants. Picnics and dances were held, often with an auction for further fellowships.

Anniversaries for alumni in good standing began to be celebrated at the Lodge. A silver medallion was struck for those celebrating one year of sobriety. A gold medallion was awarded to those who reached five years or more of continuous sobriety. A key chain was created for students and awarded to them upon discharge. The chain was to help them remember what they had learned. Later, the same design in a different shape was used to provide similar reminders to those who had participated in the Family Program and the Noble Experience. Students were told to swallow their key chains before they took the first drink or drug. Family members were told to chew on theirs before they opened their mouth.

March 1, 1985, marked a completely **new era. Little Hill-Alina Lodge became the first "smoke free" chemical dependency treatment program in the world**, they said. Mrs. Delaney felt that since she was running a healthcare facility, she could no longer permit consumption there of the most addictive substance of all time—nicotine! She encouraged other institutions to examine their policies; and many have followed suit.

On April 24, 1993, Mrs. Geraldine Owen Delaney retired as Chief Executive Officer of the Foundation. She became "Chief Executive Officer Emeritus and Founder." The same "Michael" who had developed the Family Program became Mrs. D.'s first successor, a position Michael held for over four years. He and his wife, whom we will call Ann, ran the family program from its inception in 1973. Then Michael was replaced by an interim administrator, Sister Pat, a Roman Catholic nun, who was a former student and a former staff member. And the Foundation Board began its search for new leadership. The search group had a mission to find an exceptional leader who would be well equipped to adhere to the principles recognized by Ina from her experience at High Watch Farm and A.A.—principles that were implemented and *greatly* augmented by Mrs. Geraldine Delaney.

The principles include the non-permissive approach; instruction in the benefits of Structured Living; Tincture of Time; acquisition of self-discipline; abstinence from all mood and mind-changing substances; and ongoing participation in the Fellowship of Alcoholics Anonymous. These principles–considered equally important for non-alcoholic relatives also–mean non-permissiveness; structured living; tincture of time; self-discipline; as well as ongoing participation in Al-Anon, Alateen, or Families Anonymous.

These are the principles which have caused the Lodge to believe it is firmly established as "A Place Where Hope Can Become Fact."

What is its **success record?** "**One to a customer**," was the typical reply Geraldine Delaney gave. This comment seems to parallel the assurance in A.A.'s Big Book: "Rarely have we seen a person fail who has thoroughly followed our path." Actually, in earlier days, the Lodge kept records of its success rate. The percentage of success was found to be eighty-five to eighty-seven percent. But such statistics always have qualifying factors; and that, perhaps, is why the present focus is on *each individual's* recovery, rather than upon an overall success rate.

"We think you're worth saving even though *you may not*– right now." That's a central belief and hope for students that Mrs. Delaney often tendered and expressed verbally. To the trustees of Alina Lodge, Mrs. Delaney's statement seemed very applicable to the future of the Lodge itself. The trustees were faced with Mrs. Delaney's increasing age, her declining travels and activities, and the unique nature of her ideas. They were also immersed in a racheting treatment industry battle with HMO's, insurance company resistance, and some criticisms of and by A.A.. Alina Lodge itself seemed determined to apply Mrs. Delaney's individual credo to the illustrious Alina Lodge. With an interim administrator at the helm, the trustees, staff and new leadership at the Lodge mobilized on a long-term strategic renewal plan for the foundation, staff, and programs at Alina. Peopled by a Board of Trustees (the majority of whom were former students or family members of students), the leadership remained steadfastly committed to the traditions and principles of Mrs. Delaney's program. And the team began to search for a new CEO.

The Executive Committee hired Mark Schottinger, M.A., as the new Executive Director and CEO. Schottinger began his work at the Lodge on February 8, 1998. Like Mrs. Delaney herself, Schottinger was a successful recovering alcoholic and addict. Before long, at Alina Lodge, he celebrated his 25th anniversary in recovery. He is a native of New Jersey. He is also a seasoned professional with over twenty years of experience in the leadership and management of specialty hospitals and rehabilitation centers for chemical dependency and psychiatric care. He had managed the start-up, development, and marketing of over 25 in-patient centers throughout the United States. And he had acquired a comprehensive background in clinical supervision and subspecialty expertise in creating programming for dual diagnosis, chronic relapse, long term care, adolescents, and specialized women's services.

As previously mentioned, Geraldine Owen Delaney died on July 9, 1998. In August of 1998, having been under the tutelage of Mrs. Delaney herself, Mark Schottinger assumed the post of Executive Director. Thus, an outstanding long-term successor had been carefully selected. The transition had been smooth and successful. The Delaney legacy continues. And, not surprisingly, new goals, new approaches, and new successes are being achieved.

4

The Philosophy; the Program; the Students; the Backdrop

[The author has observed a fierce loyalty among those associated with Mrs. Delaney, her ideas, and her Lodge. Alina people respect all three. They want to see continuity. And it is therefore appropriate to keep the Delaney legacy still in view. This chapter (also found in the first edition) has been retained and, where appropriate, edited only to reflect Mrs. Delaney's passing and a few other succeeding events.]

Now, just what *were* the specific ingredients of the program Mrs. Geraldine Delaney spent so many years developing?

The Philosophy of the Lodge

Old medical textbooks are said to define disease as something with reproducible, reliable, predictable symptoms. Mrs. D. often quoted Dr. David Ohlms of St. Louis as saying about alcoholism:

We doctors just don't take the time to diagnose alcoholism.

Bad treatment is worse than no treatment.

Education is the key, said Mrs. Delaney. She adapted an old saw she attributed to Dr. Stanley E. Gitlow, Clinical Professor of Medicine, at Mt. Sinai School of Medicine:

> If you want to educate, you tell them what you are going to tell them. Then you tell them what you told them. Then you emphasize it. Then you go over it all again.

Mrs. D. has written at length on some of the ideas behind the Lodge program. The following are some she emphasized.

The program of A.A. works just as well with tobacco addiction and all drugs. Whether the drugs are liquid or solid or smoked makes not one whit of difference, she claimed. She regretted that they didn't call addiction "Jellinek's Disease," for E.M. Jellinek, who popularized the *disease concept* of alcoholism. Mrs. D. did not like the name "alcohol*ic*;" nor did she like the idea of an Alcoholics *Anonymous*. There should not be a stigma or a secrecy attached to the problem, she felt. She believed "Addiction is pain plus learned relief" and that most alcoholics can recover if they are willing to do the work and not look for a "magical cure."

The "Tincture of Time" prescription, she explained, means that it takes time to rid your system of a combination of chemicals that have been stored there over the years. As to A.A. itself and what the students call "brainwashing" at the Lodge, she said:

> Of course, there are those who can go to AA and recover. But there are those who are strong and "reluctant to recover." These people need tincture of time, structured living and what the students often call "brainwashing." Actually, what is in your brain regarding the mood and mind-changing drugs, liquid or solid, legal or illegal, needs to be washed out and positive thinking put in its place.

Was there any emphasis on the power of God at Alina Lodge? Mrs. D often said:

Remember the song we sing, "Pick me up Lord—Wash the dirt off my face. Show me where I'm wrong. Put me back in my place." And the other [song], "Don't ever let go of my hand. Lord, I know I can't make it by myself and I know I can't do anything without your help. My faith gets weak, and I need you to help me stand. Don't ever let go of my hand." And [in another song] the last verse of "Up With People"—"Inside everybody there's some bad and there's some good. Don't let anybody start attacking peoplehood. Love them as they are, but fight for them to be great men and great women as God meant them to be."

If we do the work, God will help us do the impossible.

Mrs. D. titled her statement of philosophy: "A Non-Permissive Approach to Alcoholism [that] Restores Health and Hope for Alcoholics." She commented: A great many people know that Little Hill-Alina Lodge has been "graduating" students into full and successful sobriety for the past 28 plus years. This means not only abstinence from alcohol and all mood and mind-changing drugs, but also productive daily living as well. Success is based on a difficult concept in the treatment of alcoholism and poly-addiction (the use of alcohol along with other chemical substances, pills, etc.) called "non-permissiveness." This takes hard work on the part of students, family, and staff alike, but is worthwhile.

[In front of the podium in the dining hall at the Lodge hangs the statement: "I never said it would be easy. I said it would be worthwhile."]

Little Hill-Alina Lodge, its founder asserted, is the *only* "non-permissive" alcoholism and poly-addiction Rehabilitation Center in the United States.

How important is the non-permissive technique to Recovery? She said: "If we had only one hour to spend with either the alcoholic or the influential person in the life of the alcoholic, we would take the influential person because if we can get all concerned to be *non-*

permissive about the killer disease, alcoholism and polyaddiction, we can get on with successful treatment. Stated simply, *non-permissiveness in dealing with alcoholism (addiction or chemical dependency or any name you wish to give it) means not allowing 'sympathy' to interfere with 'empathy' and Recovery.* The only thing that does not work, we have found over the years, is ignoring the problem or the unwillingness to seek help. Alcoholism is not the only disease in which people sometimes are overbalanced in their thinking *by their intense sympathy;* but we do believe that the family of the alcoholic, the employer and friends of the alcoholic are more easily swayed by that 'great convincer'—the alcoholic."

She added: Over the years there have been many treatments tried. Like *some cancer victims, some alcoholics will recover spontaneously, but it is not wise to forego treatment in cancer or alcoholism in the hope that such a miracle might come forward.* All treatment must include a combination of physical, mental, emotional, and spiritual approaches. At Little Hill-Alina Lodge, the family physician or plant physician is *involved in the admission of students. A complete history and physical is done on every incoming student.* We confer with the student's physician or the Company physician before the student is admitted. This is "certification" by the private physician or Company medical personnel. We then continue as liaison with them and maintain a complete medical file on all students. Before a student is released, we again confer with the admitting physicians regarding Aftercare. We call [the residents] *"students"* because they are not bed patients at the point and time of admission though they may have been during a period of sobering up or detoxification in a hospital. In rehabilitation, they are truly students, LEARNING and RELEARNING how to live in a world oriented in the *instant* cure or instant "mood change," yet not using chemicals to accomplish this mood change.

As to medications, Mrs. D. declared: We believe *in minimum medication*, compatible with good health. We live in a *"pill-taking society."* We teach the students to eliminate the *casual approach to medication.* We want them to live free of "mood-changing" chemicals of any kind. People say it's difficult to even get an aspirin from us . . . and that's true. More than half of our students are poly-addicted, using alcohol and some other substance, the sedative drugs both prescribed and over-the-counter, though many of the young prefer marijuana and cocaine as well as alcohol.

Around-the-clock medical coverage is provided by Little Hill-Alina Lodge; and a registered nurse is on duty 24 hours a day.

Structured Living is a vital element in the non-permissive treatment of alcoholism at Little Hill-Alina Lodge. It includes regular meals and suggestions for proper eating, regular times for sessions of therapy, regular sleeping times, and guidelines for dress.

A *high-protein*, low starch, low sugar diet with added water soluble vitamins (B complex and C) is incorporated into the treatment. None of the food is fried, but rather broiled or baked and not breaded, if possible. The menu also includes fresh vegetables, lots of salad, dark bread and as little starch as possible, mainly rice and fortified noodles. Snacks are available between meals, but of the protein variety, fruit, or fruit juices. Students are *required* to eat three meals a day—a large part of their physical recovery. And they are required to take vitamins unless for some peculiar reason they are allergic or have side reactions. Regular bedtimes and rising hours, with short rest periods during the day, are observed, particularly for new people who may still be suffering from the physical effects of alcoholism.

The Lodge believes early orientation is important, and the *"buddy system"* is used. A more experienced student shares quarters with a newcomer and shows the newcomer the way around. This involves a two-way street, each sharing and learning from the other. An orientation program which discusses the treatment program is given to new students. Structured living, as developed by the Lodge, is explained; and facts and fancies about alcoholism are examined. The orientation is repeated periodically.

Students are told that it is difficult for a person who gets an unusual euphoria from alcohol and alcohol-like drugs to give up the only "problem solution" that person has found to be successful.

"The solution," they are told, has been minimal as consumption has increased, due to increased tolerance. Simply, this means that it takes more and more of the drug to give less and less effect as the disease progresses. As a result, the person is apt to try using a combination of drugs—cocktails and drinking in the evening, followed by sleeping pills at bedtime—in an attempt to calm anxiety.

Students are told *there is always anxiety following the depression of the central nervous system through chemicals.* The Lodge believes that the alcoholic obtains a greater and different "release euphoria" from the mood and mind-changing drugs than does the normal individual. This is believed to be on a "physical basis;" and much of today's research is beginning to show this is probably true. While all alcoholics are certainly not alike, says the Lodge, they do have great and multiple similarities; and ABSTINENCE is held to be the only way to arrest the disease known as alcoholism. Unfortunately, *education of the newly sober alcoholic is extremely difficult.* Hence the Lodge's EMPHASIS and RE-EMPHASIS—call it "Brainwashing" if you wish, says the Lodge. That, they say, is the best answer.

The *student is taught that alcohol always has been and always will be a central nervous system depressant*—that is, an anesthetic, a tranquilizer, and a sleeping potion. Alcohol has been so used since it was discovered. And it is still so used, not only by the alcoholic but by many people who drink. The Lodge teaches that the *body does not care how the "mood changer" enters the body, whether by gas, liquid, solid, gel, injection, tablet, capsule, suppository, cough medicine, or any other method. The body is looking for effect, not the carrier.*

Another confusing problem for students is the fact that *reaction to a drug is not the same each time.* Thus pursuit of an ideal effect is the misuse of medication, and the students need to learn this fact.

Work Therapy is also a *major factor* in re-education. Actually, many brilliant people are unable to do the simplest tasks in rehabilitation—tasks that are on the "work list." The reason? They *are* affected by the drug, alcohol. *Students are not allowed to stay on most jobs* more than a week at a time since FLEXIBILITY is necessary for successful sobriety. Students are never asked to do anything they should not do in their own homes. Rooms are kept clean and neat to conform to standards set by the Staff.

When *students first come, says the Lodge, they usually conform for a while, then get belligerent and don't.* If they really are on the road to recovery, they soon get back in line and see the reasons for, and feasibility of, doing as directed. There is the time-honored legend at Little Hill-Alina Lodge: *"Put the flowers in the vase upside down if that's what we tell you to do so that blossoms will come up brilliant."* The proposition sounds absurd, but so do many of the directives students receive. They are, however, to learn to follow directions, whatever they may think of the directions. Visitors are sometimes puzzled at the sight of the beautiful oil painting which hangs in Gratitude Hall. The flowers are in the vase upside down! The painting was done by a student who remembered. The moral is that the winners will show you the way, but you have to be willing to try it their way in order to get the benefits. This indeed involves a LEARNING PROCESS for many adults who have done it their own way for so long. And failed! A.A.'s Big Book suggests the same idea: "Some of us have tried to hold on to our old ideas," it says; "and the result was nil until we let go absolutely." The Lodge appears to believe that only through accepting discipline over a substantial period of time will the student learn to discard ineffective living techniques and learn or relearn successful ones.

Each aspect of the Lodge program has its purpose, they say. For example, students are told to *write a story of their life.* This is to promote mental and emotional peace. The requirement is not for staff benefit. It is for student benefit. When the story is finished, the student is asked to go back and underline recurring character problems and assets. Too often, the alcoholic minimizes his or her assets while accentuating defects. To *help the student gain real self-knowledge,* there are small groups for discussion. Also tapes, movies, live lectures, and one-to-one counseling. There is little recreation as that term is used today. The Lodge believes the alcoholic has been "recreating" for quite some time. Only leisure activities such as meditating, writing, and thinking are stressed, as are activities such as art and music.

One of the absolute non-permissive rules is NO FRATERNIZATION between male and female students. Women work and share with women, and men work and share with men. Men students and women students are not permitted even to *talk* with each other. Male counselors interview male students. Female counselors interview female students. The alcoholic, says the Lodge, does not need the sympathy that goes with the man/woman relationship, but rather the "empathy"— understanding—that is the counselor's stock in trade.

Family therapy occupies a large portion of the Lodge recovery program. Dr. Karl Menninger said, "In any disease, the whole family must be treated, whether it is behavior in children, mental illness, acute diseases, or alcoholism."[11]

Aftercare and follow-up are of the utmost importance; and all students are urged to attend Alcoholics Anonymous. Family is urged to attend Al-Anon and the Alateen Family Groups, and to utilize other community resources.

Last but not least, says the Lodge, is the matter of YOUR ATTITUDE. What do you really believe about the disease of alcoholism and the alcoholic when you put your head on the pillow at night. Not what you give lip service to, but what you would believe if it were your loved one. If you do not truly believe that alcoholism is a disease, and if you do not love the alcoholic in spite of it, you are urged to turn the treatment and motivation over to someone whose general make-up is such that he or she can have empathy and true understanding, rather than sympathy which is destructive. THE ALCOHOLIC CAN BE HELPED AND IS WORTH HELPING. That is a paramount thought. It parallels the current theme of the National Council on Alcoholism and Drug Dependence: Alcoholism is a preventable, treatable disease.

---

[11] Dr. Karl A. Menninger is a much-quoted and world famous psychiatrist.

All smoking for students, staff, and visitors was prohibited March 1, 1985.

The foregoing, then, are the essentials of the Lodge philosophy as they were expressed by Mrs. D. herself. And now for the ingredients of the program, to the extent not already covered.

The Program

A week in residence does not a treatment expert make! But the author did spend a week residing at the Lodge in preparation for writing the first edition of this title. The author is an active, recovered member of Alcoholics Anonymous who has sponsored more than eighty men in their recovery.[12] He himself was a resident patient in a twenty-eight day treatment program at the beginning of his sobriety. He was an alcoholic and a sleeping pill addict. He was a voluntary "guest" for two months at a Veterans Administration Psychiatric Ward in San Francisco, beginning at four months of sobriety—to the end of attempting to overcome acute anxieties, exorbitant fears, persistent shaking, and surprising physical ailments resulting from withdrawal.

Prior to his stay in residence at Alina Lodge, the author had spent a number of hours talking to a family which had benefitted from the Lodge program. He also digested tapes of Mrs. D.'s talks, articles she wrote, articles about her by others, and brochures and pamphlets on the Alina Lodge program. At the Lodge itself, the

---

[12] The author refers to himself as a *recovered* alcoholic. This is consistent with the position taken by the basic text of Alcoholics Anonymous which, in its 3rd edition, refers to the aim of the book as follows: "To show other alcoholics *precisely how we have recovered* is the main purpose of this book." See *Alcoholics Anonymous*, 3rd ed. (New York: Alcoholics Anonymous World Services, Inc., 1976), p. xiii. See also pp. xv, xvii, xxiii, 17, 20, 29, 90, 96, 113, 132, 133, 146. Many people in A.A. nonetheless speak of being "in recovery" or of being a "recovering" alcoholic. The Mom who had so much to do with this book prefers the word "recovering." She adds: "To me, we are all God's works-in-progress, ever learning, ever changing, ever choosing, ever recover*ing*—hopefully improving our understanding and application through acting as if, and acquiring better attitudes, better insights, better sobriety. Like an unfinished symphony. Recovered seems too finished to me." It's hard to challenge that!

author was well-fed and well-housed, facts which no doubt contributed to his enthusiasm. But his thoughts were not simply the product of a visiting fire chief tour. He arose with staff and students. He ate with Mrs. D., staff, students, and grads. He interviewed Mrs. D.; Mrs. D.'s immediate successor, the former C.E.O. (whom we have called Michael); many on the Lodge staff (both past and at that time); and Mrs. D.'s chauffeur (whom we have called Henrik and who also served as gardener, observer, graduate, and critic). The author attended lectures, student talks, on-site A.A. meetings, a graduate anniversary award meeting, staff interviews, grounds tours, grad luncheons, and a memorial dinner for a retiring staff member of many years experience. He talked to grads and family members, and he dived into many reading materials available at the Lodge itself. Most important, perhaps, is the fact that the conclusions the author reached were very similar to those expressed in the written materials he saw and the verbal statements he heard.

Important in the author's first review of the Little Hill-Alina Lodge program was the fact that Mrs. D. had "retired." In fact, however, her presence was still very much evident. And this had some bearing on things still being done and on changes yet to be made. But it is fair to say that, while different staff members have varying ideas and emphases, the basic program—as Mrs. D. developed and described it—was still very much the treatment approach at the Lodge, even after her retirement.

The Orientation

It would be unduly repetitious to cover program elements in this discussion of the orientation program conducted for new students. However, certain significant points were stressed in the orientation they receive. First, the orientation itself is conducted once; and then, in a later week, it is covered again for fuzzy minds that have heard it before. Initially, students are informed that they are in a place for the "reluctant to recover." They were required to "detox" elsewhere. They are told they are there for the purpose of getting their lives in order and to learn new ways of living. This, they are informed, requires discipline, structured living, the Twelve Steps of Alcoholics Anonymous, and discovering what they need to know about *themselves*. The problems of polyaddiction are emphasized. They are told clearly that smoking is banned. Also, that the Lodge is not affiliated with any insurance company or hospital network. Independence in viewpoint is claimed to be the result.

The basic Lodge philosophy was described in four ways: (1) The Lodge is based on non-permissive structured living. Students are told they have usually been sneaky in their lives and that addicts are not very good with structure or taking directions. "Good Orderly Direction" is proposed as the effective starting point for recovery. (2) Students are told they are at the rehabilitation center to receive an education. They need to learn about their disease and move away from guilt, shame, and the feeling they are bad. They have, they are told, a disease from which they can recover. Their problem does not involve a moral issue. There will be lectures, films, tapes, and group discussion. (3) The program is based on the principles of Alcoholics Anonymous. Other approaches are acknowledged, but the Lodge believes A.A. has been the most successful. Keep it simple! That is a watchword. (4) Time is the big item. A three months minimum stay is required, but students are told their stay is likely to be longer. They must spend time to learn who they are, to look at things, to write a life story, to do a Fourth Step (of A.A.) inventory, and to internalize what they find. Recovery, says the Lodge, is a life-learning process.

Some important features of the program itself are thoroughly explained. First, there is the physical recovery aspect. There is careful monitoring of physical complaints. There is a "buddy system" where a person with more time observes and helps with the newcomer's problems. Nutrition, vitamins, and limited work periods bear out the physical aspects. Next, the program strives for: (1) self-knowledge of liabilities and assets, (2) honesty with self; and (3) self-acceptance—an endeavor to let the student feel comfortable with who he or she actually is. Third, there is stress on spiritual regeneration. Students are told that, for most, spiritual values have become non-existent. There is spiritual reading just prior to breakfast. The Serenity Prayer is much used. The Lord's Prayer is frequently heard. And students keep in touch with other people through anniversary meetings for grads and thanksgiving sessions. Finally, there is the Family Program. The family learns about addiction, family recovery, support, and passing the principles on. There is a family week where students share what they are doing and issues in the family. The sharing is on neutral territory.

There are some basic program guidelines. The length of stay is more than three months. The time is determined on an individual basis according to physical recovery, past history, and the response to treatment. Recovery, not time spent, is the goal, says the orientation. Students are given a notebook and told to use it by writing down what they hear in lectures and meetings. Then, after the lecture or meeting is concluded, they are to write a critique which explains in brief what they have learned or acquired from the event. This way the counselor obtains insights which the student may not verbalize. Day by day items such as attire are covered (no short shorts for ladies; dresses and jackets with ties for every dinner). The non-smoking ban is repeated, and the fact that "patches" will be used is explained.

Again and again, students are told that time, structured living, and a non-permissive approach are considered to be the most important allies at Alina Lodge.

"Write-It" forms are a legendary part of the Lodge program. If a student wants something, the student is required to write it down with a date, the time, and his or her signature. The write-its are collected by counselors. They cover such items as drug-store supplies, haircuts, alterations, and requests to see someone or obtain some item. One student requested binoculars. Mrs. D. replied in writing, "Why?" The student said he wanted to view the wild-life (of which there is an abundance—turkeys, deer, bears, groundhogs). Mrs. D replied: "Look in the mirror. You will see all the wild-life you need." Mrs. D. concluded the student was interested in using the binoculars to see the women students.

Fraternization, verbal and non-verbal, is viewed as a *known* block to treatment. "Fraternization," says the orientation sheet, "is not only discouraged. It is FORBIDDEN. All of your emotional energy must be directed toward dealing with your own recovery." Addresses and telephone numbers may not be exchanged. After discharge, a graduate may not write to students still in residence. And only emergency phone calls from the Lodge are permitted. Again, casual use of the telephone is considered a block to treatment.

"Getting out" was very much on the mind of students and very much in the memory of graduates. The Lodge believes that this focus shifts dramatically as time and the program sink in and fuzzy thinking becomes clearer. Recovery, new tools for successful living, and a better and more comfortable understanding of one's assets and liabilities seem to be hoped-for objectives.

Little Hill starts students with this thought:

> Recovery is a process that requires time, patience, commitment, and a belief that you can get better. You have come to the Lodge because you are addicted to alcohol or alcohol-like substances or a combination. You have come to a "Place Where Hope Can Become Fact." Our rehabilitation program offers restoration of physical health, clear thinking, personal growth, and comfortable living without alcohol and mood-changing chemicals.

Some Other Student Program Features

There is to be no visiting in other people's rooms at any time. There is to be no borrowing. No places can be reserved at dining tables, and students are to sit at a different place at each meal. Conferences and personal requests are to be kept at a minimum. Possibly the most astonishing rule is the one requiring that jackets, dress slacks, dress shirts, dress shoes and ties (for men) and dresses, stockings, and dress shoes (for women) be worn at every dinner. So unusual is the sight of well-dressed men and women that the author was convinced at his first dinner that the dining hall was filled with business executives and professionals, whereas he was actually watching the well-dressed *students* conversing animatedly with each other during the meal. Mrs. D. holds this requirement to be an important factor in building discipline, respect, and self-esteem.

Listing student responsibilities, the Lodge states:

1. Each student has the responsibility for being direct and honest about everything relating to him/her as a resident.

2. Each student has the responsibility to tell those caring for him/her about any changes in his/her health.

3. Each student is responsible for clearly understanding his/her health problem and to participate actively in the designated rehabilitation program.

4. Each student has the responsibility to be respectful and considerate of all other students and staff.

5. Each student has the responsibility to honor and preserve the confidentiality of the other students both during treatment and after discharge.

6. Each student is responsible for keeping appointments and cooperating with the staff to assure continuity of care.

7. Students are expected to participate in therapeutic job assignment and housekeeping responsibilities; attend all scheduled events and three meals a day; daily complete written critiques and reading assignments; appropriately use laundry, toilet, and shower facilities; strictly observe rising and retiring hours; keep rooms in order.

8. It is the responsibility of each student to know and observe all rules and regulations as they apply to his/her conduct.

9. If a student feels that his/her rights are being violated, it is the student's responsibility to inform staff.

Students are very clear that violation of rules may find them discharged, taken to the bus stop, and sent on their way. The Lodge is a no-nonsense program.

When a student comes in, his or her medical chart is prepared and reviewed. A treatment plan worksheet is completed, with some forty "Step Four Target Areas" that include aggressive behavior, anger, fear, laziness, manipulation, procrastination, self-pity, spiritual attitude, intolerance, grief, guilt, impatience, indifference, dishonesty, depression, defensive behavior, pride, people-pleasing, listening, perfectionism, resentments, rigidity, shame, and willingness. The program, in other words, presents some tall order targets for change. Then a treatment plan is kept (and filled in) from admission to discharge and after. It covers the problem, the goal, the action to be taken, the time of report, and the date completed.

The following are some of the major parts of the program:

1. **Admission**: Students are admitted for rehabilitation by referral only. They must be certified by their personal physician or employee physician who has seen them within 48 hours of admission. They must be ambulatory, non-psychotic, reasonably well oriented, and not in need of nursing care. Students with a history of convulsions or DT's may be required to be hospitalized before admission.

2. **Treatment**: High protein, high vitamin, low starch, low sugar diet is the order of the day. Good nutrition is considered the basis of good physical and emotional recovery.

3. **Routine**: Regular hours for education sessions, eating, sleeping, rising, and work therapy provide the basis for relearning self-discipline. The treatment is termed "the firm

sell" on the theory that most treatment programs have tried the "soft sell," without adequate results.

4. **The Life Story**: The student's "life story" forms an important part of the program. The student is told to put down on paper memories of the major points in his or her life, beginning with childhood. The memory is to involve description of feelings, emotions, and attitude. The student is told to be honest, that no one will read the story, and that there is no one to impress and no one to conceal from. There need be no search for hidden meanings or deep-seated causes—just a description of things that happened, how the student felt and reacted, and what the attitudes were at the time. The story is to be put aside for a full day and then read at one sitting if possible. There can be post-scripts; and the material is also used as resource material for the Fourth Step Inventory. In addition to covering childhood and school years, the story is to cover adult year work patterns, dating, marriage, children, sexuality, values, death or loss, and drinking and drug behavior. The author observed that at various points, a student presents an "I am" story to the students assembled; and presumably some of the insights gained in the written life story are a part of the verbal story.

5. **Group therapy**: At least three to four regular Educational Sessions are held each weekday, and three are held on Sunday by members of the professional staff and volunteer therapists. Therapy sessions range through tapes and lectures by non-alcoholics and alcoholics, small group discussions, special lecture sessions by clergy, doctors, psychiatrists, staff, and/or former qualified students sharing their experiences. Students must take notes. After each session, students are required to close their notebooks, in which they were asked to record ideas they liked and ideas they disliked. Then they must write a short note covering this point: "What did I get from this session for *me*?" Frequently, statements about what the student heard that was disturbing provide food for further investigation into his or her thinking. Also, the writing encourages the student to "listen" and to "concentrate." Films are becoming more important in treatment, and the Lodge's film library is

extensive. Literature and reference books are supplied for study guides for the student's personal inventory and for the inventory for the spouse. Books on alcoholism, together with numerous pamphlets and charts, are recommended for reading. Two examples can be found in Appendices One and Two. Many are given to students and family. In general, the approach to therapy is one of "reality." The focus is on what the student is today as a result of the student's past—the student's assets and liabilities today; the short-term and long-term goals the student can set up within the limitations of his or her present age, health, and situational problems; and how the goals can be attained. It is believed that such investigation creates planning with flexibility; and considerable accent is placed on learning to discipline oneself in small things as well as large. A.A., Al-Anon, and Alateen are explained, reviewed, and tendered as the best supportive therapy in existence.

6. **Recreation**: This item is minimized on the theory that "Operation Head Start" is a cram course and that recreation can be postponed. However, brisk walking, reading, and relaxing in the sun are suggested activities between sessions. Interestingly, there are art and music sessions for all.

7. **Daily Moral Inventory**: Students are challenged to look for self-pity, self-justification, self-importance, self-condemnation, dishonesty, impatience, hate, resentment, false pride, jealousy, envy, laziness, procrastination, insincerity, negative thinking, vulgar and immoral and trashy thinking, and criticizing.

8. **Goal of Treatment**: The alcoholic is encouraged to attain total abstinence from alcohol and alcohol-like drugs (mood and mind changers) and to use inner resources, help from friends, and A.A. therapy to face the realities of their lives. Mood and mind changers are presented as curing nothing. The Lodge quotes Ronald Fischer, Professor of Experimental Psychiatry and Pharmacology at Ohio State University: "Not only do tranquilizing agents not cure, though they may help to produce a less demanding and complaining alcoholic; they can induce irreversible brain damage." Fischer added that "Thorazine," the

most widely used tranquilizer in the Western World, "may be expected to produce irreversible brain damage if more than 400-500 mg. is administered for an extended period of time." The Lodge warns that physicians and institutions alike should consider this fact. Liver damage from drugs is a real threat, says the Lodge. And Mrs. D. adds, "It has been my experience that chemical 'instant cures' for the alcoholic, regardless of the name—prescribed or over-the-counter—are detrimental to the goal of total abstinence from alcohol and often retard emotional maturity."

9. **Results**: How is success measured? Can it be measured just by total abstinence and statistics, asks the Lodge (though its statistics are considered excellent if sobriety alone is the criterion)? Students who stay until they are advised to leave are said to have excellent potential. Evaluation studies at five years can be helpful, but other emerging problems of life can be the deciding factor. In their addictions, students have learned that pain can be "dissolved" temporarily by chemicals. Perhaps the most difficult part in an ongoing rehabilitation program is combating the symptom that "Calmness is just a swallow away." Society tells the person who is not continuously calm and anxiety free that he or she must get relief. The Lodge believes the alcoholic or addict cannot afford such relief and must therefore relinquish the only solution he or she has learned for his problems. The Lodge believes its role is to help the alcoholic learn he or she can adequately cope with life's problems, personal characteristics, and inadequacies without the use of "mind altering" drugs of any kind. If the alcoholic must have an "addiction" (pain plus learned relief = addiction), says the Lodge, "we hope he will transfer to a 'people addiction' and an addiction to the 'positive living today' philosophy." Alcohol and other tranquilizers tend to be "synergistic" (one plus one equals four or even six, rather than the expected two). On the other hand, people who live in the day can be synergistic, because one person plus one person trying to recover will bring multiple satisfaction never achieved by "mood changers." The goal is a well-adjusted, productive, and healthy life without chemicals, coping daily with the realities of life.

A jaunty Lodge poem provides a suitable conclusion to the program summary:

A heart full of thankfulness,
   A thimbleful of care;
A soul of simple hopefulness,
   An early morning prayer;
A smile to greet the morning with,
   A kind word as the key
To open the door and greet the day
   Whate'r it brings to thee.
A patient trust in Providence,
   To sweeten all the way;
All these, combined with thoughtfulness,
   Will make a happy day.

Aftercare

Adequate and careful planning for discharge is a vital part of the program. Follow-up letters, telephone calls, the providing of community contacts, consultation periods at regular intervals, "In-Patient Refresher Periods," and alumni groups to bridge recovery are all provided. Alcoholics frequently need longer time, even than the long-term rehabilitation center time. They are told of a study at Johns Hopkins Medical School that reported "Memory functioning was markedly impaired *after* withdrawal from alcohol." The Lodge concludes this means very close observation over a longer period. Also that many so-called "pure" alcoholics, and all those polyaddicted, make little mental and emotional progress during the first three weeks at the Lodge. The majority of students have had hospitalization, some A.A. exposure, and frequently psychiatric treatment before admission. This indicates, says the Lodge, "that those coming to us are the sickest of the lot." Also, there are frequently omissions by the patient, family, employer, or referral agent because of fear that admission will be refused. Such omissions can jeopardize lives; and the Lodge believes the alcoholic has lied too much too long.

Alina Lodge believes that recovery from alcoholism is a continuing process, and that residential care is the beginning of sobriety. Time away from mood and mind changing drugs is another element of recovery. Continued recovery also includes good diet, adequate rest, education about the disease, and acceptance of the disease. Self-discipline that will aid the goal of living life to the fullest as a non drinker in a drinking society is vital. Students are asked to work with their counselor to write a plan that applies to them. They are encouraged to plan physical continuity—adequate diet, relaxation, exercise, and sleep. There is to be treatment for existing medical problems such as diabetes, high blood pressure, etc. Routine physical checkups are encouraged. Students are asked to plan for changed relationships with family, friends, work, the community, and specific social and recreational activities. They are challenged to improve mental, emotional, and spiritual health. They are asked for specifics. They are asked to think of vocational and educational goals.

For many students, further structured living in selected half-way houses is encouraged after their departure from the Lodge.

The Family Program

The Lodge has always been dedicated to the understanding that alcoholism/addiction is a "Family Disease." This is a disease that has direct impact on the well-being of those intimately or even simply acquainted with the addicted person. In many ways, the Lodge points out, the attitudes and behaviors of the relatives of alcoholics/addicts parallels that of the chemically addicted individual. Spouses, children, parents, and other relatives are usually uninformed or misinformed about the nature of the problem and rarely have any positive outlet for ventilation or guidance regarding the problem.

In 1973, the Lodge began a formal program to provide accurate information about addiction and healthy support for family members coping with the disease and its effects on them and on their loved one. In October of 1994, the (Alina) first onsite facility in the country opened to provide residential therapy for the relatives of the Lodge's students in treatment.

The family receive information about the Family Program a few days after the student is admitted. No telephone contact with the student is permitted except in an emergency, as determined by the CEO or designate. Visiting the premises is allowed only with staff permission after the student has been in treatment for at least twenty days. If appropriate consent forms are signed by family and student, a "buddy" is selected for the family. The "buddy" is a relative of an alumnus of the Lodge who lives in the area of the family involved. That buddy is a resource to lend support and answer questions in the early phase of care. The buddy also introduces family to the 12 Step Fellowship meetings, particularly Al-Anon, Alateen, and Families Anonymous—also to open A.A. meetings.

Sunday is Education Day. The day is so named in contrast to "Visiting Day" to keep family mindful of their purpose at the facility. Education Day consists of required sessions and individual conferences with staff. Sessions include an introductory class on the nature of alcohol and alcoholism (See Appendix One). Another session deals with issues directly pertaining to the relatives of the students. These issues include the progression of the disease in the non-addicted person, and that person's expectations, feelings, attitudes, communication, and family denial.

Family are also given pamphlets. One is titled "What Can I Do To Help?" (See Appendix Two). Another is titled, "Releasing With Love."[13] Releasing with love is defined in several ways. One says this "detachment with love" means being:

---

[13] The pamphlet's author is Neil Uptegrove.

objective, but not indifferent;
flexible, but not indecisive;
firm, but not hard;
wise, but not clever;
patient, but not resigned;
strong, but not overbearing;
resolute, but not stubborn;
compassionate, but not indulgent.

"It means," says the pamphlet, "separating the personality you love from the disease you despise; accepting the afflicted one unconditionally as an individual of worth and dignity, while steadfastly rejecting the destructive influences of alcoholism on yourself and on the family members in your care. It means caring enough to relinquish your fantasies and fictions. It means foreswearing anger, resentment, fear, recrimination, self-justification, false pride, self-condemnation, and self-pity. It is a course of constructive independence, not a license for retaliatory self-indulgence. It is an assertion of your human rights, not a usurpation of those of the alcoholic. It is a tool for serenity, not a weapon for retribution."

A pamphlet widely distributed to students and family details "The Progression of the Family Disease of Alcoholism in the Non-Alcoholic Spouse." It covers the following points:

1. **Change: Becoming Restless as Change in the Drinking Pattern or Behavior Begins**. The non-alcoholic spouse is embarrassed, irritated, or uneasy as unusual behavior episodes become more frequent. "What will people think?" He or she may even doubt themselves if others think lightly of, or even applaud such behavior. "Maybe I'm a wet blanket." The spouse begins to feel real concern over the partner's drinking; for uneasiness grows with excessive drinking emerging on the part of the alcoholic. The spouse looks for reassurance that there is no problem. He or she may ask the drinker to take it easy or watch out for drinking too much. The non-alcoholic spouse often relaxes if told: "I can handle it;" or "Oh sure! No

problem!" Also the spouse is elated and reassured when the alcoholic "behaves well." Moderation in drinking has "solved" the problem! And the denial of alcoholism in the family has begun.

2. Blame: Looking for the Cause or Something to Blame for the Negative Changes. The non-alcoholic spouse is dismayed, baffled, or angry when drinking episodes continue. The spouse wonders why the alcoholic is not controlling the drinking this time. "What went wrong?" "I thought we agreed. . . ." The spouse begins to think up excuses to explain the alcoholic drinking. "They shouldn't have been drinking on an empty stomach." "They were very tired and uptight." "They are entitled to cut loose once in a while." The spouse is bewildered, alarmed, and angered by the alcoholic's forgetfulness or even negligence toward responsibilities. Confusion and self-doubt occurs over the alcoholic's convincing denials about events occurring during "blackouts" (period of alcohol or medication induced amnesia when the alcoholic has no recall of behavior). Self-doubt increases. The non-alcoholic spouse is peppered with accusations by the alcoholic that the spouse or family is the "cause of it all." Quick denials and convincing alibis leave the non-alcoholic spouse wondering where reality lies. The non-alcoholic spouse is bewildered and frightened as "Jekyll and Hyde" personality changes in the alcoholic become more vivid. Sudden and unpredictable reversals in the alcoholic's mood and character leave the non-alcoholic spouse fearful and confused, wondering, "What did I do this time?" "Maybe they have emotional problems." "Maybe they are crazy." And the "drinking problem" has become a major source of discord in the relationship.

3. Control: Attempting to Control the Drinking and Behavior of the Alcoholic. The non-alcoholic spouse tries to control the alcoholic's drinking. The spouse manipulates social schedules, duration of "cocktail hour," dinner time, selection of guests, types of entertainment, and even friends in the hope of restricting the alcoholic's drinking. The spouse resolves to "try harder" with each failure. The spouse feels it is a duty to "do something" about the drinking. Bottles are hidden, diluted, or emptied. The alcoholic is asked, "Can't you see what you are doing to yourself and the family?" The spouse distracts (encourages hobbies, sports), promotes "geographic cures" to move away from the problem. There is nagging and threats. The spouse assumes more and more of the alcoholic's routine responsibilities; takes over an increasing number of tasks previously handled by the alcoholic—balancing the checkbook, household chores, and child care because "somebody has to do them" and the alcoholic "can't be trusted." The spouse becomes resentful over increasing burdens, with a growing sense of martyrdom and self-pity. "Why me?" "Poor me!" "If only they . . ." The spouse "walks on eggs" to avoid upsetting the alcoholic. Family members unite in extreme efforts and deceptions to avoid controversy or confrontation they feel might "set the alcoholic off again." Fearing for reputation and financial security, the non-alcoholic spouse goes to great lengths to maintain appearances of "normalcy." This is often an attempt to buy time for the problem to "work itself out." Finally, the spouse is terrified or hurt over the increase in emotional and/or physical violence. The alcoholic's seeming ruthlessness, callousness, and intensity of emotion are frightening and shocking. And disillusionment and frustration increase.

4. **Defend: Setting up Personal Defenses**. The non-alcoholic spouse seeks opportunities to avoid contact with the alcoholic (e.g. works more hours, goes shopping more often). The spouse "invites" compliments from others to bolster self-image (e.g. does volunteer work, joins committees, coaches teams). Ego mounts in defense of reality. The spouse becomes self-indulgent. "She or he can't do this to me." There may be irrational spending sprees, compulsive eating, or extramarital involvement. The spouse withdraws from usual social activities with close personal friends and relatives. Communication with the "outside world" shrivels. The spouse considers separation or divorce. Half-meant threats of the past now loom as the only alternative. "Damned if I do, damned if I don't" syndrome surfaces. And a senses of hopelessness emerges.

5. **Despair: Negativism and Despair Become Predominant Attitudes**. The non-alcoholic spouse undergoes a profound personality change. Sense of humor, feeling of creativity, and sense of personal identity, direction and purpose are crushed beneath the weight of the disease. A sense of failure and rejection mount. Powers of concentration and decision making fail as self-esteem and self-confidence shrink. The spouse has fallen into a love/hate relationship with the alcoholic. True concern for the alcoholic alternates with anger and disgust. Sex becomes a weapon or is abandoned. Guilt over ugly thoughts toward the alcoholic. The spouse loses original spiritual values. Spirituality, which the Lodge calls a feeling of belonging, erodes. Self-preoccupation grows. The spouse has increasing emotional and physical aliments. Sleeplessness, tremors, uncontrollable crying, temper flare-ups, digestive upsets, head and back aches, circulatory problems, migraine-like headaches, allergic reactions, asthma attacks and skin disorders are a few examples. The spouse experiences growing morbid fears and imaginings. The spouse is haunted by vague and irrational terrors, fantasies of suicide, serious doubts of one's own sanity ("I think I must be going crazy"). Life has lost all meaning or value.

6. **What's Next**: Either a lifetime in the grip of bitter resentment, guilt, and self-doubt, or gradual recovery through acceptance of alcoholism as a family disease and a readiness to accept help for yourself. The help that has worked best for most is participation in the Al-Anon Family Group Program. You do not have to experience phases 2, 3, 4, or 5 if you receive guidance from people knowledgeable about alcoholism: Al-Anon Family Groups, Alateen, Alcoholics Anonymous, Adult Children of Alcoholics, The National Council on Alcoholism, Local Alcoholism/Addiction Agencies, Families Anonymous.

There is a similar pamphlet outlining the family disease in the parents of chemically addicted children. To avoid undue repetition, only the major points are set forth below:

1. **Family Disease**: Watching the child abuse alcohol and drugs, allowing negative consequences to occur without our interference, is simply too painful for most of us. So we take over the child's responsibilities, protecting and compensating for the child's behavior. We do what we are "supposed to do" as parents. However, these behaviors have the reverse effect of what we intend. Our actions will keep the addiction going through what has been called "enabling." This over-protective, overcompensating behavior shields the addict from the consequences and symptoms of his/her disease. We have fallen into "the parent trap." The points following may help parents identify the ways in which chemical addiction has changed their lives, their attitudes, and their feelings.

2. **Change**: Parents may observe a changing peer group ("My old friends are boring"); changes in school, work, or recreation ("My teacher/boss is unfair!"). "I'm just trying to have a little fun;" changes in physical appearance ("Everyone dresses/looks like this; it's the new style"); changing attitudes at home ("You can't make me!" "It's my room!"); the development of legal problems, including citation for drunk driving ("It wasn't my fault."); drinking or other drug paraphernalia or activities ("I don't know where it came from!"). Parents just dismiss the feelings of concern; and denial has begun.

3. **Blame**: Parents blame the child's lack of responsibility on "adolescence." They blame the influence of the press or other media. They blame their own inadequacy or lack of parenting skills. They blame the child's behavior on "emotional problems." The parents blame one another ("You're too strict/lenient/inconsistent"). Changes increase. Tension grows. So does conflict between parent and child and often between the parents themselves.

4. **Control**: Parents are involved in endless advice giving, scolding, arguments, repeated warnings, and punishments. They often try to regulate friendships and socializing. They try to occupy their son or daughter's time. They try to maintain peace ("If only we could get along better"). They try to cover up for the child.

They utilize guilt, anger, and shame to maintain order ("Look what you are doing to your mother/father/sister/brother!"). Parents struggle with each other for authority ("Don't be so hard on him/her."). Parents become overly restrictive of other children in the family (setting curfews). They try to buy happiness (Buy him/her a car, apartment, clothes, etc.). They eavesdrop. The consequences may mean headaches, digestive disorders, skin problems, respiratory difficulties. Disillusionment, fear, guilt, anger, and tension become emotional mainstays for the household.

5. **Defend**: Parents often fight over the "right way" to handle the addict. They seek opportunities to avoid contact with the addict or each other. They justify their inability to discipline or set consequences for unacceptable behavior ("Why bother! It's like talking to a stone wall."). They overcompensate to bolster self or family image (Excessive volunteering or preoccupation with external appearance). They become verbally or physically threatening to the spouse or addict. They withdraw from socializing. They begin lying to relatives and friends. And, as communication diminishes and isolation grows, feelings of anxiety and hopelessness increase.

6. **Despair**: Parents undergo profound personality changes. They experience a love/hate relationship with their son or daughter. They lose spiritual values ("Why would God let this happen to us?"). They have increasing emotional and physical ailments. There are morbid fears and imaginings as to answering the phone, possible accidents involving suicide, overdose, criminal acts, or automobiles. Parents experience separation, divorce, or sexual problems.

7. **What's Next**. Parents can learn the facts about this disease. They can construct a support system to help them make sound decisions. They can learn to stop enabling. They can develop a "First Aid Kit" of resources available: doctors, detoxification or rehabilitation centers, emergency squads, members of Twelve Step programs, or private counselors. Learn the criteria for admission. Have telephone numbers for the resource list.

The foregoing, then, can be helpful education features for families. There is also a question and answer discussion session. Arrangements can be made for one-to-one conferences, sometimes with the student included. A student has lunch and visits with a relative for about two hours. Only two visitors are permitted on a given Education Day.

Residential treatment is tailored to individual needs. Relatives come for up to one full week. They attend sessions with their student; and, in the case of spouses, cohabit during that time if agreeable to both parties. No more than two or three relatives of one student attend at a time. If there is more than one needing to participate, additional family weeks are scheduled. The schedule consists of daily lectures, two discussion periods, audio/visual material, and written assignments. The week begins with an orientation session for all. The first therapy session involves each person introducing himself. All, including staff, give a personal history, taking from twenty minutes to over an hour, depending upon the need. Other session topics are based on the expressed needs by the participants plus an assessment of needs by the counseling staff. One-to-one conferences are held as well. Assignments are, for the most part, voluntary and may be shared in group or individually or not at all. Participants decide when they are ready for encouragement and support. As with Education Day, topics discussed reflect personal need. Discipline, structured living, looking at self, and involvement in 12 Step Fellowships are all stressed.

There is ongoing aftercare for family members in the form of couples' therapy, alumni events, special education days, workshops, conferences, and telephone support indefinitely at no charge.

No person may visit who has had any alcohol or other mood or mind changing chemical within twenty-four hours of arrival. Any person using mood or mind-changing medications or pain-killing medications such as tranquilizers, anti-depressants, muscle relaxants, or antihistamines is not allowed on the premises. No smoking is permitted at any time by anyone anywhere on the premises of Little Hill-Alina Lodge.

Family members are to make a written list of all positive as well as negative aspects in their current situation with the alcoholic. The list is in writing so that the points will not be forgotten in discussions with counselors.

Basically, only items approved by the staff may be brought in to a student. No food is to be brought in. No food is to be sent for birthdays or holidays. Photographs must not be brought without clearance because the Lodge has found that snapshots of persons or events often stir up unsettling emotions which may lead the student to depart prematurely. Letters to students are encouraged. Visitors are not to engage other students in conversation; nor to correspond with other students or their relatives; nor are addresses and telephone numbers of other students or their visitors to be exchanged. Relapse, jail, and even death have sometimes resulted from such activity. Students are not to greet nor to say good-bye to the family in the parking lot and are not permitted near the visiting automobiles. The stated purpose of almost all these rules is to prevent distraction of the student and keep structured living, self-discipline, and the education goals in focus at all times.

5

Spirituality and Twelve Step Programs

Finding and Trusting God

"Spirituality" has endured some strange twists since the founding of Alcoholics Anonymous on June 10, 1935. Yet A.A.'s approach to things "spiritual" seemed quite simple when the First Edition of A.A.'s basic text was published in the Spring of 1939. Recall too that Geraldine Delaney had contacts with A.A.–and certainly with the ideas of Bill and Lois Wilson–that went back to early days. She certainly was familiar with what A.A. Co-founder Bill Wilson wrote in his basic text:

> We never apologize to anyone for depending upon our Creator. We can laugh at those who think spirituality the way of weakness. Paradoxically, it is the way of strength. All men of faith have courage. They trust their God. We never apologize for God. Instead we let Him demonstrate, through us, what He can do (p. 81).

Famed as the author of A.A.'s "Keep It Simple" idea, Co-founder Dr. Bob Smith put spirituality even more concisely in his personal narrative:

Your Heavenly Father will never let you down! (p. 193).

Dr. Bob further remarked that the whole program could be simmered to "love and service."

And the portion of A.A.'s Big Book which sets forth the Twelve Steps has always contained the following challenge:

> Without help it [alcohol] is too much for us. But there is One who has all power—That One is God. May you find Him now (p. 71 of the First Edition)!

Today's A.A. literature, many treatment people, and a good many AAs themselves are fond of saying that A.A. is "spiritual and not religious." But the veteran A.A. historian Mel B. writes:

> Typical is, "Our program is spiritual, not religious." If pressed for what the program's actual definition of *spiritual* is, however, it's doubtful that many AA members could explain (Mel B., *New Wine*, p. 5).

Here's what Mrs. D. had to say about all this:

> My father was a Baptist. My mother was a Methodist. My brother was a Presbyterian, and my third husband was a Roman Catholic. I started out as an atheist.

> Religion is about how you set the table. Spirituality is belief in a power greater than myself that I call God—and living as my God would approve of.

> The spiritual approach at Alina Lodge means the students must know their own God. If they don't believe, they are to follow Good Orderly Direction. That's what I got from believing in a power outside of myself. Know myself. I'm the problem.

> We should try not to interfere with God's will. I need to ask God for guidance. I can't run the show.

I am happy in any house of God built to thank God for His goodness to us. How they sing or how they worship is not important. If I get anything out of the service, that is enough.

I thank God in the morning for a good night's sleep. I used to get on my knees when I prayed, but I can't now. I thank God at night for a good day. I need help, and God seems to provide it.

We allow a priest to come and say Mass each Sunday for those who want to attend.

Prayer is needed in life. If you don't talk to a life-saver, how can they know about you. I talk out loud because I realize if I don't talk out loud, I may let things slide.

God will answer if we listen.

Go to a meeting. Maybe you are just the person God wants there.

I don't know about you, but I wouldn't want to meet my Maker half-bombed.

The author found the Lodge well-sprinkled with spiritual sayings and inspirational books. The Serenity Prayer, the Lord's Prayer, the Prayer of St. Francis, and Mary Stuart's Prayer were there. Also, in the dining area, there were a number of issues of *Guideposts* that were available for general reading. There was a spiritual meditation each morning with reading from the lectern in the dining room. Spiritual power was stressed as a requisite for recovery. Spiritual values involving the vital ingredients of "love" are everywhere mentioned. The expression "Higher Power" (hardly a favorite with this author and virtually unknown in early A.A.) was noticeably less used than at so many A.A. meetings of today and in today's Twelve Step literature.

Little Hill-Alina Lodge did not and clearly does not want to qualify as a religious or Christian treatment program. People of many faiths, Protestants, Roman Catholics, and Jews, are demonstrably present as students, family, and graduates. Roman Catholic priests seem to have been a part of the advisory people who frequent the Lodge; but there was no emphasis at all on the Bible, Jesus Christ, or Christianity. When the author was introduced at a luncheon, Mrs. D. applaudingly mentioned his books on the spiritual roots of A.A. in the Bible, the Oxford Group, and Christianity. She had already endorsed one of the author's books; and the author was invited to, and did, address the students on the spiritual roots of A.A. during the author's stay at the Lodge. He had none of the discomfort one sometimes feels in Twelve Step atmospheres when the roots of A.A. in the Bible, the Oxford Group, and Christianity are mentioned.

Particularly refreshing in the "spiritual" arena was Mrs. Delaney's open-mindedness and desire to learn at her very advanced years. She had many of the author's titles on the history of early A.A.'s spiritual roots and successes in her office during the time of my visit. More than once she had made or written the following comment; and she graciously and humbly allowed it to be placed on the cover of the author's *The Oxford Group & Alcoholics Anonymous:*

> Dick: I have your books, New Light on Alcoholism, The Akron Genesis, Dr. Bob's Library, Anne Smith's Journal, and The Oxford Group. You write exceedingly well and simply so that folks like me can understand and enjoy.

I was and am most grateful for Mrs. D.'s willingness to read, discuss, and endorse my many years of research and writing on A.A.'s basic ideas from the Bible, Quiet Time, the teachings of Rev. Sam Shoemaker, the practices of the Oxford Group, Anne Smith's Journal, and the literature of the early program. Even more that she enthusiastically invited my writing of her biography and made possible the extensive interviews of her.

The author was given the following during his stay at the Lodge:

CAN WE TRULY SAY THE "OUR FATHER"

I cannot say "Our" if my religion has no room for others or their needs.

I cannot say "Father" if I do not demonstrate this relationship in my daily living.

I cannot say "Who art in heaven" if all my interests and pursuits are earthly things.

I cannot say "Hallowed be thy name" if I, called by His name, am not holy.

I cannot say "Thy Will be done" if I am unwilling to give up my own sovereignty and accept the righteous reign of God.

I cannot say "Give us this day our daily bread" without expending honest effort for it or by ignoring the genuine needs of my fellowmen.

I cannot say "Forgive us our trespasses as we forgive those who trespass against us" if I continue to harbor a grudge against anyone.

I cannot say "Deliver us from evil" if I am not prepared to fight in the spiritual realm with the weapon of prayer.

I cannot say "Thine is the kingdom" if I do not give the King the disciplined obedience of a loyal subject.

I cannot say "Forever" if I am too anxious about each day's affairs.

I cannot even say "Amen" unless I honestly say, "Come what may, this is my prayer."

Alcoholics Anonymous and the Twelve Steps

It seems to be a hallmark of treatment centers today that there is stress on A.A. and the Twelve Steps. Most possibly pay some homage. Many require attendance at outside A.A., N.A., and C.A. meetings. Some invite A.A. speakers to come and share. The Big Book is often studied; A.A.'s *Twelve Steps and Twelve Traditions* is studied; and the Steps are studied. And the question might be: Does the Lodge do more?

To begin with, Mrs. D. had been sober fifty years, stemming directly from her participation in Alcoholics Anonymous. She avowedly claimed to be a "member" of A.A.—a fellowship which really does not have "members" as such. She was a close friend to Bill and Lois Wilson, co-founders of A.A. and Al-Anon, respectively. She knew Co-founder Dr. Bob. And her brother Oscar was an AA "sponsored" by Bill Wilson. Oscar got sober in 1941. Mrs. D. got sober in 1947 and was very proud of that fact.

AAs are invited to come to the Lodge with their groups and put on a regular A.A. meeting. Grads, visitors, and guests often give "drunkalogs" that are A.A. oriented. And the Big Book and Steps are admiringly mentioned and carefully studied. Unlike many centers, the Lodge guides students through all Twelve Steps. It urges them to get sponsors and go to meetings immediately after discharge. Mrs. D. endlessly said and repeated the statement that Bill Wilson frequently told her that "doing" A.A. meant: "Don't drink. Don't drug. Go to meetings. Listen. And SHUT UP!"

As can be discerned from the literature at the Lodge, the fellowship of Alcoholics Anonymous, the Twelve Steps, the Big Book, the "Twelve and Twelve," and writings by Bill Wilson are very much in evidence. The programs of A.A., Al-Anon, and so on are referred to a great deal by Mrs. D. and the staff. Study of the Big Book is stressed. And the usual A.A. plaques, slogans, and sayings can be found at almost every turn.

The Lodge boasts that it is based on A.A.; and, for the most part, that appears to be a reasonable claim. The A.A. ideas have a special "warmth" in an atmosphere where they are espoused by a long-term sober member who befriended, knew well, and supported the concepts of founders Bill W. and Dr. Bob.

Mrs. Geraldine O. Delaney

6

Reflections, Recollections, Renewal

[The author himself was very much involved in a treatment center where he had been a patient. He came there right out of grand mal seizures at an early A.A. meeting. He completed the twenty-eight day program. He attended after-care men's meetings, alumni meetings, meetings for the older patients, and a special discussion group of alumni led by "Joe" and open to all. The author served as a volunteer briefly. He conducted "Step Study" meetings for patients for many months. He was the founder and first secretary of a weekly men's A.A. meeting held on the premises for men-patients and attended by many AAs. He attended alumni forums, dinners, celebrations, and picnics. He frequently ate his dinners at the rehab long after his discharge. And he was well-acquainted with the director, knew a number of counselors quite well, and even invited two to speak at A.A. meetings where he was secretary. I therefore feel it is fair to say that I was an enthusiastic, albeit very sick, patient, alumnus, volunteer, and participant in a highly reputable treatment center. I went there at the recommendation of my physician, who was a specialist in treating alcoholics and addicts.]

The point is that I had a real sense of the feelings of the center's leadership, staff, facilitators, patients, and alumni. That continued for several years; and many of the patients asked me to serve (and

I did serve) as their A.A. sponsor. I also believe I had a good sense of how quick local physicians and others were to send their difficult alcoholism and addiction cases to our center.

But, the extensive, direct involvement and the loyal passions of Alina Lodge people is something I hadn't seen at "my" center. Many of the Alina staff were graduates and loyalists. So were the visiting alumni and alumnae. So were some of the trustees I met. So too seemed the tributes to Mrs. Delaney and her lodge that abound–tributes from Betty Ford, Father Martin, Abraham Twerski, presidents, priests, popes, professionals, actors, and entertainers. There was something special there! And it warrants a deeper look into the reminiscences of some very directly informed about the premises.

I believe the "renewed" Alina does add up to a bright future. There are past analyses, endorsements, awards, and recoveries that have put Alina at the head of the pack. There are proposed changes and new plans that will help it meet today's treatment battles fully armed and prepared for victory. And there are the loyalists–those who liked Mrs. Delaney of old, those who liked Mrs. Delaney when old, those who felt the transition was successful, those who felt the transition needed improvement, and those who have worked with great determination– who will probably see, from this review, a very new, very renewed, and very refreshing Alina Lodge where hope can truly still become fact.

Let's tread some of the past experiences again. Then let's hear from the new administration. And let's provide a good description of what can now be found at Geraldine Owen Delaney's Alina Lodge in this new millennium.

Geraldine D.

Mrs. D. "collected" owls. She claimed she did not *collect* them. Rather, that people give them to her. Whatever the source, however, owls abound on the premises she frequented—big owls, little owls, porcelain owls, owls made of shells, fuzzy owls, toy owls. Owls everywhere! She said they have no particular significance; but the following poem was popular with her:

> A wise Old Owl sat on an oak.
> The more he sat, the less he spoke.
> The less he spoke, the more he heard.
> Why can't we all be like that Wise Old Bird?

The poem reminds the author of a favorite saying in the Oxford Group, precursor of A.A. The Oxford Group attributed it to a Chinese proverb:

> God gave a man two ears and only one mouth.
> Why don't we listen twice as much as we talk?

A.A. pioneer Clarence Snyder used to say:

> Prayer is talking to God, and meditation is listening to God. God gave us two ears and one mouth; and that should tell us something.

> You know from experience that when you run around, are in a hurry and get busy, you need to get physically quiet so that God can speak to you, and you can hear Him. God says, "Be still and know that I am God."

It seems that quiet time, meditation, and listening are part of A.A.'s biblical legacy that passed down to the Lodge. Meditation was a definite part of the program at the Lodge. So was a stress on prayer. And Mrs. D. certainly emphasized *listening*. Over and over she shouted that Bill Wilson told her to "shut up and listen." Whatever kind of listening either Mrs. D. or Wilson were thinking of, Mrs. D.'s program is designed to keep the student focused, self-disciplined, and attentive. The absence of distractions, the taking and keeping of notes, and the making of critiques all bespeak listening. Perhaps even the owls!

There are many reminiscences of Mrs. D—Isms. The following impressed the author as being significant:

I didn't say it would be easy. I said it would be worthwhile.

You can get used to hanging if you hang long enough.

The first hundred years are the hardest. After that it doesn't make any difference.

She has about as much chance [of recovery] as flying a kite in a coal mine.

"To each his own," said the lady as she kissed the cow.

I've always liked men better than women ever since I found out they were different.

The family undoes in 5 minutes what it takes us 5 months to put together.

If I had only one hour to spend with alcoholic or family, I'd spend it with the family. It would do more good.

I'm always good. Some days I'm better than others.

There must be an easier way to make a living than the way I'm doing it.

With two hot water bottles of Canadian whiskey strapped between my legs, honey, I was popular! [Mrs. D. on her prohibition supply route across the Canadian border]

If alcohol did to you what it does to me, you'd be an alcoholic too.

If I tell you to put the flowers in the vase upside down, put 'em there.

Take off your intellectual pants and sit down.

Do you want him/her if they never change.

My name is Gerry and I'm an alcoholic. I'm awful nervous so I think I'll sit down. [Mrs. D.'s first A.A. talk]

You look like the south end of a bus headed north.

I've managed to avoid it so far. I think I can make it the rest of the way. [Mrs. D. on housework]

Love is understanding whether we approve or not.

You'd make coffee nervous.

You never can tell by the looks of a frog how far it's going to jump.

I think I'll bring you in for the long, long term program—5 to 25 years.

New alcoholics are the greatest liars in the world. They lie to themselves and they lie to everyone else.

Tears are the floodgate of the soul.

Our students are the worst of the worse, and they turn out to be the best of the best — if they stay sober!

Lord, keep my memory green. If I picked up another one, I'd be a dead duck.

I certainly don't want to meet my Maker half-bombed.

Mrs. Delaney once summed up her tough attitude in this way: If you have to have a disease, alcoholism is the best one to have. When I'm talking with a parent who is lamenting over the child's problem, I ask if the parent would rather the child have aids, or syphilis, or cancer. To lie to the alcoholic is tantamount to death. You might as well kill him. If you say, "Oh no, you're just fine," that's a lot of malarkey. So I just keep telling the truth. I remain tough because I know it's the right thing to do. [As to hurting anyone's feelings:] I don't care if I hurt people's feelings. I'm not running a popularity contest. The important thing is do I like myself? Do I approve of what I'm doing. It isn't whether *you* approve. Your approval isn't going to help me one bit. It's when I can look in the mirror and say, "You did the right thing." But, you know, people come back and they tell me, "I hated you. I just despised you. And now, I know I wouldn't have gotten well any other way." Those are the things that make you know you're doing the right thing. It isn't what you think. It's what I know to be true. It's this: knowing yourself, and then either accepting, or changing.

Some Thoughts by Mrs. D.'s First Successor

Michael fashioned the Family Program at the Lodge after Mrs. D. sent him on visits to other recovery facilities. He is no longer at the Lodge, but was Mrs. D.'s immediate successor. The author spent substantial time with Michael and attended several lectures by his wife Ann, who headed the Family Program. Much was covered that is not recorded here, but the following points deserve attention.

Michael believed that the students were at the Lodge to look at themselves—their disease and their unmanageable lives. This examination with a minimum of distractions so they can hold up a mirror to themselves and receive a thorough education in A.A. He declared that the program requires *time*. Not merely learning, but applying; not just hearing about the disease, but gaining competence to live the program of recovery.

He said there are weekly Step meetings. Students are involved with counselors minimally every two weeks. Their "write-its" cover a wide range of typical problems such as credit and bills, letters from home, child problems. The "write-its" enable students to remember issues when they consult counselors. The "write-its" give focus to questions, and even possible answers. Michael declared the spiritual focus is non-stop. He defined spiritual in terms of reliance on something outside of self. He also said spirituality, from his viewpoint, includes willingness to follow, to conform to group conscience, and to develop a belief in something greater than self. As students begin to thaw from their spiritual bankruptcy, he said, they develop the ability to "get on their knees." They are urged to develop a personal belief based on their own belief system. Michael's theory was that "coming to believe" is part of the grace of God, not a therapy issue. He did subscribe to Mrs. D.'s concept of "Good Orderly Direction" which means [in terms used by A.A. "Founder" Professor William James and A.A.'s spiritual teacher, Rev. Sam Shoemaker] "acting as if."

Michael believed Mrs. D. exuded spirituality. She was, he said, charismatic, re-assuring, and comforting. She was not a member of an organized religion, but she did attend Sunday School as a young person. He thought she believed that God need not be the God of organized religion. He sometimes thought of Gerry as a "female General Patton." His respect for her was immense, as is that of staff members. He saw the Lodge itself at the cross-roads. It had been self-sufficient and had not depended upon insurance companies or institutions. But times have changed. A major source of referrals in the past were "detox" facilities. With Mrs. D.'s retirement and the drying up of many treatment facilities, he believed aggressive marketing of the Lodge program was needed. But several Board and staff people raised questions about his lowering of discipline, sometimes termed "liberalism," and his feeling that discipline perhaps became harsh and punitive in Alina's later years. Michael saw the Lodge as firmly grounded, uniquely free of debt, highly successful, and in a position to be a beacon for treatment as a new generation of leaders takes hold—leaders who, for the most part, were trained by or under Mrs. D. and have been working for her for long periods of time.

Conceding that the Lodge frequently speaks of the "reluctant to recover," Michael nonetheless contended it also has a primary care dimension. This means, he said, that there is now a minimum stay of two months for those entering residential care for the first time. He emphasized that the Lodge program is not alone for multiple repeaters or chronic relapsers. Now that there are fewer short term programs, he says, "we are trying to help in that department and move away from the view that everyone is here forever!"

Mary

Mary had resigned just before the author arrived at Alina. She had been associated with Mrs. D. for a long time—first as student, then as counselor. Students sometimes jokingly called her a "lifer"—a term derived from the prison scene and perhaps coined because of Mary's long tenure at the Lodge, her seeming toughness of attitude, and her round-the-clock presence and devotion. The author was privileged to attend the dinner given in her honor at the time of her resignation from the Lodge, and to hear accolades from Mrs. Delaney, her colleagues, Foundation Trustees, and alumni.

The author then spent an entire day interviewing and having lunch and dinner with Mary; and she had much to say about the history, philosophy, program, and possible future of the Lodge.

Much of the material she mentioned has already been covered, but Mary's remarks provided much perspective as to what the Lodge was all about. There is a joke about her. At the beginning of her service on staff, she was often seen carrying towels around the premises. One person said she believed Mary was carrying towels because she had disobeyed the rules and would *never* be permitted to leave the Lodge, ever! But her resignation ended speculation about that.

Mary pointed to a special feature at the Lodge: Detox does not occur there. The normal detox period for the alcoholic is three to five days, she said; but it is ten to fifteen days for addicts. And in this period, there must be precautions against seizures and other complications. This often means administering dilantin and phenobarbital. It also meant, for the Lodge, that the initial period of recovery should begin in a *detox facility* where medical supervision was available during the critical period. Mary recalled the early days when facilities merely housed "warm bodies breathing." She herself began recovery in 1976 and says she nearly "shook to pieces." And she was angry! She entered the Lodge at a time when the program lasted six weeks for student alcoholics under fifty-five years of age, with twelve weeks required for those over fifty-five or dually addicted—usually to such drugs as valium, librium, or sleeping pills. Vital signs were taken four times a day.

The Lodge program was taking shape step by step and student by student. Many of the rules and recovery ideas came from experiences with the students. The "buddy system" was in place when Mary arrived. A roommate was with the new student twenty-four hours a day, attending meals and sessions. This lasted two weeks and was partly for safety reasons. The student did what the buddy did; and it taught each to think of another. It also enabled evaluation of the buddy as well.

"Art on Saturday" began. Students were provided with crayons and told to draw. This helped fill the day and teach patience and communication, but it also enabled Mrs. D. to "read" what they were drawing—for example, when pictures were distorted.

The one-hour-at-meals rule had also been instituted. Mrs. D. told students, "You don't know how to talk." Consequently, all students sat at tables for an hour. They were virtually compelled by that length of time to engage in conversations with other students. And the students were watched! Mary likened the behavior of some to that of a swan. The swan appears tranquil above the water surface, but the feet are usually churning. So too the student, and students' feet were watched. Counselors also observed the people with whom a student chose to sit at mealtimes. Sometimes there would be an "executive table" where those who felt self-importance tended to congregate; but such selective pack behavior was quickly sensed and promptly terminated.

Both on Mary's entry and when the author visited, infraction of the rules was serious business. Any student who deliberately chose to miss meals, miss sessions, walk with students of the opposite sex, pass notes to them, or walk off the premises knew that in doing so, he or she faced the fact that the consequences of violating these known rules might well mean discharge from the Lodge. As Mrs. D. said, "Every action has a consequence." Many students have been to treatment facilities where there was a swimming pool, exercise, and access to phones, friends, and potential sexual partners. But this was not to be at the Lodge. Students were not allowed to walk anywhere but designated areas—areas for men and designated areas for women. For their own safety, students were not to run or jog, but simply to walk briskly ("wogging" it is called). Phone privileges were severely limited; and students were told to focus on the "Big Book" of Alcoholics Anonymous (the basic text of that Twelve Step Fellowship). They were told, "You are the problem, and you are the solution, and the answers are in the A.A. program."

Mary explained "Music." Students were given rattles, cymbals, and records. Mary remembered crying when they sang "Amazing Grace" and "Lord, Teach us to Pray." Singing is still very much a part of the activity. The author observed it at an Anniversary Night where an alumnus told his story after five years of recovery. The author observed it at an alumni luncheon and on another occasion. Songs were up-beat.

Mary remembers thinking, "I'll never drink again if I can get through this day." No student saw a counselor until three weeks had passed at the Lodge. As Mary put it, "Nobody was home *up there.*" Meaning there was only confusion, forgetfulness, and a racing mind "up"in the brain during early sobriety. She recalls lectures on honesty, hopelessness to hope, despair, deceit, dishonesty.

A theme in Mary's day at the Lodge and at the time of the author's visit was "Who am I?" The author attended an "I am" session where two different students explained to the student body who they had been before coming to the Lodge. Mary became impressed with the idea that she had been "a nice person who had become something she never intended to be." She learned instead that she was sick, getting well; not bad, getting good.

No kids allowed! Under thirteen, that was. There were, of course, reasons; but the prohibition on children was often misunderstood. No children were allowed as visitors, in part because others had no children and felt left out on visiting days. Also, many students could not handle their children; and they were taught they had to face *consequences* for their previous actions—parents or not.

Large notebooks were required in Mary's student days, and the author noticed plenty in the lectures he visited. Students were to write what they were getting out of the lecture and what they retained. The notes were not critiques. After the lecture, however, students were to "shut their books" and do critiques. The critique contained the name of the lecture topic, the counselor giving the talk, the date, and the time. The critiques helped staff to identify shaky hands and goofy concentration, said Mary. They showed whether the student had been listening or not. The critiques also illustrated attitudes.

Just prior to their discharge, students went to see Mrs. D. It was a big event. Mrs. D. said to Mary on the eve of her departure: "You think you have been doing well. I don't. You have broken no rules, but you have done nothing. You haven't changed. You haven't mentioned A.A. once. If you go for a job, what will you say you were doing during your stay here?" In response to this upbraiding, Mary stayed on two more weeks. Then she was told, "There is nothing you can't do. You have great talents. But you can't stay sober. At the end of these eight weeks, we give you a 'key ring.' But you are not finished. You are going to drink again. So you go home, and go to A.A. meetings." Mary went home, but her job plans did not work out. She was filled with anger and self-pity. Before long, she went to a liquor store. She bought two cans of Manhattans and drank. She passed out. Then she called Mrs. D. to see if she could come back. She was told by the person who answered that she must stay a whole year. She objected. Mrs. D. said, "Put Mary on the phone." Mrs. D. asked, "What are you willing to do?" Mary replied, "Anything. But not one year. I only had two drinks." Mrs. D. responded, "I don't care." Mary was permitted to return.

After four months of her second stay, Mary asked Mrs. D. if she could leave. Mrs. D. answered, "You have as much chance of success as flying a kite in a coal mine." Mary asked to stay on and become a trainee. She remained at the Lodge for over two decades—a reason students called her a "lifer." She started by making beds. She cleaned "johns." Then she was subjected to another of Mrs. D.'s ideas—"Tincture of Neglect." Mary needed healing time. She became the "alter ego" of Sister Pat, the Roman Catholic nun who had been both student and then staff member (and then returned temporarily as *interim leader* and consultant). Mary took broken people and worked with them "all the time."

Mary opined, "Alina Lodge is a spiritually blessed place for the sick and suffering alcoholic. Money has never been the objective. I was taken the second time free. She [Mrs. D.] worked the buns off me. Every building was paid for before the first shovel went into the ground. Help always came. At times, we didn't know where finances were coming from. We just believed."

Of Mrs. D.'s spiritual condition, Mary said, "She [Mrs. D.] has been in search of a God of her understanding for most of her life. She has found Him in her believing. Many priests have blessed her at the Lodge. Father Peter (a Benedictine priest) called her 'Mother.' He had intended to visit her before he died; but he had to go to the hospital for heart trouble. The night he died, Mrs. D. called him although she had other plans. She cared."

Mary is a proponent of half-way houses. She has recommended one in New Jersey and another in Florida for women graduates. "The Lodge," she said, "may not put the last piece in your puzzle, but it will give you a big chunk of it." There is a half-way house in Minnesota where its people meet the graduate student at the plane, take the student under their wing, and help the student set up an apartment. Follow-up structured living is important, she believed.

The Lodge favored living in day-tight compartments. According to Mary, "We take care of 14 out of 24 hours. What do you do with the rest?" The key is filling up one's life with structure. "One day at a time," was Mrs. D.'s frequent remark.

Mary concluded with these things about Geraldine D.: "She gave her life totally and completely to this work. She is the most brilliant and most dedicated woman I have ever met. She knows more about alcoholics than anyone I ever knew. She knows about valium and librium and phenobarbital. She stresses rest, good food, structure, discipline, and the non-permissive approach to rehabilitation. Often when a student asks for something, she says 'No you can't. Now what do you want?' Structure, discipline, and non-permissiveness are the hallmarks of Mrs. D.'s approach," said Mary; and, quite clearly, the Lodge premises bespeak the application of Mrs. D.'s ideas.

Staff, Employees, Others

Joe [A fictitious name]

Joe was a senior counselor. He was also the highly thought of counselor to the graduate student the author interviewed. Regrettably, Joe was not on duty until the end of the author's visit; but he seemed to have a deep understanding of Mrs. D.'s techniques and compassion.

It was Joe who explained to the author the meaning of "Grambo"—the moniker the students hung on Mrs. Delaney. Joe showed the author the "Grambo Slugger"—a baseball bat with that name and the further phrase, "Attitude Adjustment Tool." Mrs. D. sometimes carried that bat around the dining room, tapping her hand with it when some student was out of line at meals.

Joe also showed the author the "Tire Whomper"—a billy club Mrs. D. kept in her office, supposedly for self defense, but mainly to brandish at some disobedient student. Joe had seen her put on a show seemingly to terrify the student, wag the Tire Whomper, and then give him a hug. If she got a tough one, she would wave the billy club and say, "You don't scare me one bit. If you were that strong, you wouldn't have succumbed to alcohol." She would say, "Get in here [to her office]." Then she would chew the student out. Often the student would cry, and she would feed him man-sized tissue, saying: "Tears are the flood-gate of the soul. I'll do what I can to help."

Joe's conclusion about Mrs. D.'s spirituality was expressed as follows: "She is the instrument of a Higher Power and allows herself to be used as much as she can. She has enthusiasm, and that word is derived from 'God within.' She does not pay lip-service, but rather service to her Higher Power. She is really a lonely person because she has sacrificed so much of her life in other areas."

Joe believed Mrs. D. frequently sought God's guidance on matters pertaining to the conduct of the program and her dealings with staff, students, and grads.

Frank [A fictitious name]

Frank was a counselor who came to the Lodge from A.A. about fifteen years ago. His training as a counselor included spending three months doing what the students do. He sat with counselors during their work. Later, he took the work required for certification as a substance abuse counselor. He felt that the certification training which meant the most to him was the information he received on the pharmacology aspects of addiction.

Frank was enthusiastic about the buddy system. He said it involved placing an older person with a new person. The older student looks after the newcomer's needs, explains the program, and develops a friendship. In two weeks, and for the first time, the student meets his counselor.

There is great emphasis at the Lodge on waiting for the fog to lift and meeting no distractions—no distractions from the other sex, from exercising, television, or reading (except for such an item as the Bible). Discipline is stressed—dressing up for dinner, eating by row. Also highlighted at the Lodge is its Family Program. Families are encouraged to stay a week in residence. They are asked to list their expectations and issues with the student. Frank underlined the drug-free life the Lodge advocates—starting with "No smoking." There is, he pointed out, an emphasis on A.A., on nutrition, on sleep, and on alumni groups.

He left the author with this interesting prediction: The student leaves the Lodge and returns to the community a *calmer* person, better able to *communicate* with other people.

Helen [A fictitious name]

Helen was a mature counselor with an M.A. degree. She had worked elsewhere as well. In the brief time the author spent with her, he could sense her great concern over the importance of other addictions which she believed trigger a return to alcohol and drugs.

For example, she pointed to such addictions as anorexia, bulimia, sex, gambling, and debt. Also to such issues as hidden gay or lesbian preferences. She believed that if these items are not unearthed and addressed by the student, the student may leave the premises alcohol and drug free, but unable to resist a return to his or her substance of choice by reason of frustration over other addictions and issues that have been left unresolved.

She pointed to the possibility of referral to other places for such problems. She added that, because of her particular sensitivity and training, staff members at the Lodge often send people to her where there *is* another problem.

Henrik [A fictitious name]

Henrik was the "other" person (other than Mary) regarded by students as a "lifer." Henrik is devoted to the garden; and the Lodge premises flourish with beautiful lawns, extraordinarily healthy flowers, and delicious vegetables. But Henrik is more than a gardener. He was Mrs. D.'s chauffeur. He frequently traveled with her to assist her. He often escorted dismissed students to the bus and discharged students to their place of transportation. And he is a graduate.

Henrik had an abundance of experience with Mrs. D., with her personality, and with her convictions. He was able to describe the philosophy and program of the Lodge in just a few words. On the way to the airport with the author, Henrik had these things to say:

> We want what we want when we want it. Mrs. D.'s answer is discipline, structure, and "humble pie." Even the "write-its" exemplify the discipline she teaches. She hammers away, and she gets results, he says. The Lodge addresses the "Sin of omission," as he puts it. "The student often doesn't tell everything; nor does he or she listen to other students." The Lodge also deals with the "Disease of entitlement." "The world is mine," says the student. "I've had a rough deal." "It's someone else's fault." They want to get well, but on their own

terms, proclaims Henrik. And she cuts them down to size. Many, says Henrik, are "quarter-turners." He states that some students figuratively just turn the TV knob a quarter turn. The picture gets fuzzy. They get used to it. The picture seems normal. But there's much more to the matter of getting a proper picture.

The Others

The Lodge is well and thoroughly staffed. The author heard some excellent lectures. One was delivered by the former CEO's wife, Ann. She headed the Family Program and worked with families and students. She is articulate, well-informed, and has an effective presentation of subject matter. Another male-counselor delivered an orientation talk which seemed to the author to give the students a clear and simple picture of the philosophy and program. There are two nurses on duty at all times, and the author frequently sat at meals with these staff members and found them thoroughly conversant with the program the Lodge conducts. All these people sat for the full hour required of students at mealtimes and certainly got a feel for what the students were doing at meals and during their reports for medications, tests, and other medical problems.

There were still others with whom the author had little contact; but the group with whom he ate, to whom he listened, and whom he interviewed presented a consistent and complete picture of what Mrs. D. and the Lodge offer in terms of long-term treatment. Also, table guests at Mrs. D.'s table (where the author sat) were often alumni who offered their comments at mealtimes.

Mom

[Following are the reflections of a mother whose son was a student at the Lodge. She also participated fully in its Family Program. She tells how she and her husband felt and what the Lodge accomplished.]

When our twenty-two year old son was arrested, having been caught purchasing cocaine, we were stunned. Our child had never been a problem. We couldn't believe it. He called from jail. Shame, embarrassment, secrecy dominated our thinking. We called a lawyer.

At the suggestion of the lawyer, and as a condition of his release from jail the next day, our son entered a twenty-eight day rehabilitation program nearby. Counseling, lectures about drug and alcohol abuse, plus his abstinence from substances, assured me that my child would accomplish his stated desire, to "learn new habits" and "adopt a new life style." Hungry for information, I attended helpful meetings offered to families.

These meetings introduced a concept I had never heard before: People who seem compelled to use mood and mind altering substances are not simply stupid. They are ill and need help. As symptoms of addictive illness were explained, I began to understand. I could identify symptoms my son displayed. I could see that we as a family had gradually come to react to him in typical and protective ways.

Within days of his return home from that rehabilitation facility, he drank beer and used pot. Confronted with our need to know why he did not stop using, he sobbed that he couldn't. Our family began to realize that we had a major problem and didn't know what to do. For everyone's safety, we were able to have him readmitted to the nearby rehab. The counselor there, Phil [not the counselor's real name], advised us that he knew of a place that could help our son. That place was Alina Lodge.

Both Phil and counselors from the Lodge helped us see the wisdom of offering our son a choice: We would offer him rehabilitation time at Alina Lodge; or he must live elsewhere, not in our home. By the grace of God, he chose the Lodge, and Mrs. D. assured us that it was all right that he had made the right decision for all the wrong reasons.

How I remember the relief I felt that my son was in a safe place for at least three months. I could picture him getting well there, and began praying for that.

Mrs. D. had told us that she and her staff could do more to help our son than we could. That was a concept I couldn't grasp. I had spent my life working to understand and help my son. I loved my son. These people were all strangers.

One of the suggestions made at the Lodge is that we try to "act as if." To me, "acting as if" meant trying on a suggested behavior or belief; practicing it; and, if appropriate, watching it work; and eventually adopting it as my own. I tried "acting as if" Mrs. D. was right: acting as if I was able to release my son to the Lodge and give him to the staff for them to care for. I attended the required family sessions and cooperated with suggestions such as refraining from using alcohol.

Letters from our son revealed that he too was expressing evidences of "acting as if," trying on new behaviors and beliefs. A letter written two months after his arrival stated, "Even though I'm in a place where I have virtually no rights, where the rules are more strict than boot camp, I am more happy than sad. I am happy to be free from *drugs* and *alcohol* and *cigarettes*. I'm most happy to be free from myself. The empty feeling that created the need for the above was the thing that needed fixing most. I have an alternative that . . . [the twenty-eight day rehab program] didn't get across to me. It's going to take more time, but I can tell it's there for me."

Then, as Christmas was nearing, almost four months into his stay, my son sent a poem he had read at the Lodge. It was called "A Bend in the Road." "It means so much to me," he wrote, "I want to share it with all my family." And this is the poem (Author unknown):

> When we feel we have nothing left to give,
> And we're sure that the "Song has ended,"
> When our day seems over and the shadows fall
> And the darkness of night has descended,
> Where can we go to find the strength

To valiantly keep on trying.
Where can we find the hand that will dry
The tears that the heart is crying?
There is but one place to go and that is to God
And, dropping all pretense and pride,
We can pour out our problems without restraint
And gain strength with Him at our Side.
And together we stand at life's crossroads
And view what we think is the end.
But God has a much bigger vision.
And He tells us it's ONLY A BEND.
For the road goes on and is smoother
And the "pause" in the song is a "rest."
And the part that's unsung and unfinished
Is the sweetest and richest and best.
So rest and relax and grow stronger.
LET GO AND LET GOD share your load.
Your work is not finished or ended.
You've just come to a "BEND IN THE ROAD."

"I am coming to realize," continued our son, "that life without this kind of optimism, and without faith, is more trouble to live than it's worth. It makes my worries seem so small and keeps me on the journey, which is where I want to be because, as Mrs. D. says, 'The destination doesn't bring us happiness; it's the journey that does.' I am at the bend in the road. That is my gift from God and from you. I really am grateful to be here and to have parents that care so much for me and give me an opportunity like this. Thank you and Merry Christmas."

We families were urged to keep our Christmas giving to our students simple: perhaps two or three gifts, like a pair of socks or mittens or a sweater. We are always quite extravagant with gifts, and it was difficult for us to restrain our giving when our son was accustomed to an ample bounty. Mrs. D.'s simple reminder was, "Whose birthday are we celebrating anyway?"

Not being together as a family throughout the holidays was hard on us all. Imagine my reaction to my son's note, "I had the most wonderful Christmas of my whole life!" Yes, I felt relieved and happy: Yet there was also a deep pang I felt because I had nothing to do with making his Christmas the best ever.

Other letters came, some reminding us that acquiring sobriety is hard work. There were times that scared me terribly, when he was discouraged and wanting to walk away from the Lodge. Yet he knew that if he did, he would not be welcome back either at the Lodge or at home not clean and sober. I kept a picture card and sent one to him with the poem "Footprints in the Sand." [The following is that well-known poem.]:

> One night a man had a dream. He dreamed he was walking across the beach with the Lord. Scenes from his life flashed across the sky and he noticed two sets of footprints in the sand, one belonging to him and the other to the Lord. When the last scene of his life had flashed before him, he recalled that at the lowest and saddest time of his life there was only one set of footprints. Dismayed, he asked, "Lord, you said that once I decided to follow you, you'd walk with me all the way. Why, at the troublesome times of my life, the times I needed you most, would you leave me?" The Lord replied, "My precious, precious child, I love you and I would never, never leave you. During your times of trial and sufferings when you saw only one set of footprints. . . That was when I carried you."

It seemed to me that when the road became really rough and God seemed to have abandoned us, it is then that God was simply carrying us.

The following summer, our son left the Lodge far more equipped to confront the big world with his experience of sobriety. In my mind I carry a picture of my son at that time. He had spent almost a year at Alina Lodge learning about himself, about the disease of alcoholism, wanting to recover, trying suggestions, yes, "acting as if." The Bible verse in Ephesians expresses the picture best, "Put on the full armor of God. . . ."[14] He had acquired God's armor at the Lodge and was ready to venture into the real world now. He seemed to value his sobriety enough to make it the number one priority in his life. If so, time would tell—he would choose to wear that armor as he had learned.

Anyone who has loved an alcoholic knows what it means to me and my family to have a son (brother, husband) who has celebrated eight years sobriety, goes on to earn a college degree, has a good job he enjoys, is a healthy, enthusiastic husband, a grateful alcoholic who participates in the fellowship of Alcoholics Anonymous, and a joyous guy folks love to be with. Just for today, I am who I am. A grateful Mom! [And Alex has now been sober for 13 years.]

For me, I have become able to say with conviction that Mrs. D. was right. She and her staff at Alina Lodge have done far more for my son than I ever could. Those we love the most are the very ones we are least able to help.

I am among the uncountable, quietly grateful, who pray that the program Mrs. D. spent forty years of her life developing will continue to be honored, nurtured, and used for recoveries of sick and hurting alcoholics and their families.

[The author can say from personal knowledge and continuing friendship with "Mom" that neither the continued success of her son, nor the retirement and passing of Geraldine Delaney have deterred her from service to the Lodge. She helped in the hiring of a successor to Mrs. D. She helped in reshaping the new administrative approach. And she is helping for long-term planning and funding in this new century.]

---

[14] Ephesians 6:10-11, King James Version, states: "Finally, my brethren, be strong in the Lord, and in the power of his might. Put on the whole armour of God, that ye may be able to stand against the wiles of the devil."

Alex, a Student Alumnus

To protect the anonymity of this male student and his family, the author has called him "Alex." That is not his real name. He is a young, clean and sober, highly successful former student of Little-Hill Alina Lodge. Alex is the son of Mom, whose story appears above. The author spent several hours with him at his family's home, met his parents, and joined all three in a family dinner. The story is an inspiring example of what the Lodge has done for one former alcoholic/addict, for his parents and siblings, his employer, and the bride of his recent marriage. Most of the story is just as Alex related it. [And Alex is now a father!]

At first glance, you would conclude that Alex must always have had his act together. He had everything. Successful and loving mother and father. Successful and loving grandparents. Well educated. Good looking. Trim. Wanting for nothing. Except self-esteem, that is. He considered himself a "putz." As a young man, he knew he was a good athlete; yet he always felt he was the worst. He also felt that he could never live up to his own grandiose expectations of success for himself. While this is not the reason he drank, it does explain why, for him, drinking and using drugs felt so good. It did a good job of helping him escape from himself, giving him false confidence and comfort he was so sorely lacking.

As one A.A. activist on Maui puts it, there are no victims—only volunteers. As Mrs. D. puts it: "You drink for one reason, and one reason only. You drink because you like what it does to you." As Bill Wilson's medical mentor Dr. William D. Silkworth put it in the A.A. Big Book, "Men and women drink essentially because they like the effect produced by alcohol. The sensation is so elusive that, while they admit it is injurious, they cannot after a time differentiate the true from the false. To them, their life seems the only normal one." That was the case with Alex.

The "normal" life, for this Lodge student, actually meant that fear ruled his life. Alex said: "Everything I did was from fear. Obsessing over a girl friend with fear of rejection; fearing to quit smoking though I wanted to; fear of not living up to my own expectations of what I considered to be success; fear of not 'looking good.' I felt I needed a beautiful woman and success and wealth I could not possibly attain. Expectations and reality were too far away from each other. I was like a rubber band with my expectations at one end and reality on the other. The great distance between the two created tension and stress that kept my self esteem very low."

Alex's drug of choice is "pot" (marijuana) which he used much and "loved." He says he did well with it—"considering" and likened it to alcohol, with control. When he got into cocaine, though, all control was lost. "I couldn't even try to stop," he says about cocaine. "By the grace of God, I was 'busted' in a 'sting' operation by the police," he recounts. This twist of fate, he says, did for him what he could not do for himself—reveal to his family the extent of his troubles. Upon receiving the call from Alex in jail, his parents allowed him to stay overnight before bailing him out. He dropped out of the college he was attending and voluntarily went off to a twenty-eight day rehabilitation program near his home.

In rehab, Alex "played the game" well. Upon leaving, he was deemed "most likely to stay sober" by his peers. But that was not to be. Like so many alcoholics, Alex was very good at acting and, with the pressure of authority (the law) off of him, he quickly returned to his drug of choice *and* cocaine (which had now become more like his drug of choice).

Realizing Alex had returned to old behavior, his parents—with the help of his rehab counselor—called a family meeting for intervention. With great courage, they presented him with an ultimatum: Go to long-term treatment (Alina Lodge); or be cut loose from the family in every way. In no time at all, a very frightened Alex, he says, was off to the Lodge after a drying out period at his old rehabilitation center.

"For the first month I thought someone was going to tap me on the shoulder and apologize for the mistake and send me home," Alex recalls. "Then, for the next two months, I carefully studied how I was going to convince them that I was well enough to go home."

Some at Alina were model students. Alex was not. But he does have a great many detailed recollections of his stay there. Ultimately, he became one of the many miracles. He can look back and realize how much he was helped by Mrs. D., the Lodge program, and the staff. He recalled with conviction: "It saved my life. I wouldn't be sober today without it. It seemed to educate my family about the disease. It got my mother active in Al-Anon for a while, and even more in her interest in Alcoholics Anonymous. Today, when sobriety gets tough, I always have a clear picture of Geraldine D. and my mother to set me straight. I usually get myself to a few extra meetings then."

"The Lodge," says Alex, "stripped away externals and left the raw shell of what I had been. They took everything away. You had to ask permission for everything. With all this clutter removed from my life, I was forced to look within. The pain that I felt when I saw myself was my motivation to do the only thing possible—to change! The Lodge enforces your bottom [the point where the alcoholic concedes to alcoholism and concludes he or she has had enough and will do anything necessary to recover. He surrenders!]."

Alex says the Lodge emphasized the importance of the Twelve Steps of Alcoholics Anonymous. They had him write out the Steps. They made him *live* the principles, he says. Intellectualizing them came later. "At first, however, I felt like a caged rat. I wanted to get out. You don't know when you are getting out. You are always concerned with the formula for getting out; and I thought I had it figured out."

A major turning point in Alex's recovery occurred after about three months. He had an office visit with Mrs. D. She said to him, "You have nothing spiritually. You blow like the wind, people-pleasing. And in response, you cry. What are you going to do?" "What should I do?" he inquired through tears.

Mrs. D. replied, "Start taking suggestions. Pray. Get honest. Try doing all that your parents taught you as a child. Get on your knees every day and ask for God to let you see His will and to give you the power to carry it out. Write the events of the day in your journal."

Lacking faith, Alex struggled with his understanding of God. His counselor had told him of an acronym: Good Orderly Direction as a starting point. Alex said he understood Mrs. D.'s suggestion that he had to get honest; and he started to have the willingness to try not to lie.

He says about prayer: "As I recall, my first prayers were something like this: 'God, if there is a God, let me see your will and give me the power to carry it out.'" He says the very next day he was walking with his friends telling stories. A lie popped into his head. He hesitated and realized that he had the option to tell the lie or not to tell it. "I chose not to," he says. "It was the first time God had influenced my life that I could remember, and I immediately felt good. God had answered my prayer and had given me the power to carry out His will. It was a spiritual experience that was the beginning of a faith in something other than myself."

Alex says that simple spiritual experience blossomed for him at the Lodge as time and time again he had the willingness to do what he had now learned was God's will for him. "Today," he says: "I still have the option to do God's will in almost every aspect of my life. I sometimes choose not to do His will and take mine back. Quickly, though, I feel badly about myself, which makes me realize exactly what I have done. And I know that a meeting, a phone call, or simply a quick amend will make me feel comfortable again. When I am going to meetings regularly, talking with my sponsor, working on good relations with my wife, and staying on top of my daily chores and career work, I stay comfortable with myself. It's that simple."

Alex was presented with the Alina Lodge key chain (a symbol of successful completion of the Alina Lodge program). He decided to go back to his home town. The very night he got home, he went to an A.A. meeting and said, "I have just left the Lodge, and I need a sponsor." He got a sponsor. And even though he had thought he had done all the Twelve Steps at the Lodge, he did them again with his new sponsor. He brought with him a good understanding of the principles and worked hard on practicing them in all his affairs.

The principles he said he learned were: (1) the willingness to turn his will and his life over to the care of God; (2) to make a fearless moral inventory; (3) to make the faith leap of Steps Six and Seven, become aware of his character defects, and have the ability to choose whether he would allow the defects to surface; (4) to understand that he himself did not have the power to accomplish that; and (5) to help others.

A full-fledged A.A. program became a part of Alex's life. It still is. He takes commitments like making coffee and being a group treasurer at A.A. meetings. He gives leads (shares his experience, strength, and hope) at meetings. He calls his sponsor as needed. He sponsors men and takes them through the Twelve Steps. He attends A.A. Conferences.

After Alex left the Lodge, he returned to college, received A's in his courses, graduated, and got his teaching credential. He got married. He teaches science and loves it. He believes it is OK not to be the business tycoon he had once expected of himself. His self-esteem (self-approval, as he puts it) is up. He uses prayer and meditation in his daily life. He proclaimed to the author, "I am a fisherman. I have food on the table, a house, and time to fish. I do well as a teacher. I love kids [and, as mentioned, he is a dad now]. I am a blabbermouth about science and love to teach it. I am extremely happy in my marriage. I would say I am not so much God-centered as faith-centered. I can't say God put me here on this earth to teach kids, fish, and stay sober; but that's my situation."

Alex continued: "I have a life that is better than my wildest dreams, and I couldn't imagine it any different. I am so lucky to have been given the gift to go to the Lodge at a time in my life that could have been ruinous. To have been able to learn from one of the greatest AAs to ever live, Mrs. D. To have the gift of sobriety and to share it. To have been so empty only eight years ago and to be so full of life and love and purpose today. To stay sober one day at a time and to be happy."

There was a touching postlude to the author's visit with Alex. The interview with Alex had taken place at the home of Alex's parents. Alex's dad came home from work. His mother had prepared a wonderful meal. We all sat down together. Before the meal, Alex's dad asked that we all join hands; and we did. The family said this prayer together: "Come Dear Jesus and be our guest; and let our daily bread be blessed." We all squeezed hands. The prayer is part of a long family heritage from Switzerland.

Alex's mother drove the author back to the Lodge. As her car pulled out of the driveway of the parents' home, I looked at the lighted windows in the family home. There stood Alex and his dad, framed by the window, and waving. They kept waving. We waved back. This is a family ritual. They call it the "big wave." Alex's mother says it is a way of letting the traveler know you are thinking of him or her. The wave back means you are thinking of that person too. She says you know by this exchange that you are all on the same "wave length."

And now again, after thirteen years of sobriety, Alex is part of that whole family ritual. He is on the same wave length. A delightful young man, savvy about sobriety and savvy about A.A. A credit to what God, Mrs. D., the Lodge program, A.A., and his family's support have helped him do. A testimony to his own determination to change, to be satisfied with his abilities, and to stay clean and sober. All these instead of a life that could otherwise been wasted. A life that could have ended in despondency, jail, or death.

7
New Kid on the Block

"What Happened, and What It's Like Now"
by Mark Schottinger, M.A.,
Executive Director of Alina Lodge

[Mark Schottinger is the New Executive Director of Alina Lodge. He's the replacement for founder Geraldine Owen Delaney. He's not a "kid"–referring to the popular singing group of today. But he's new on the block at Alina. Maybe he felt exactly like the new kid, considering Mrs. D.'s 90 years of age, 50 years of sobriety, and 40 years on the "block" at the Lodge. Mark took over a prestigious facility with a seasoned staff, loyal to, and supportive of, Mrs. Delaney's ideas. Mark's position faced him with unusual opportunities, demanding challenges, and very unique problems. Here's how, mostly in his own words, he viewed the new job.]

There were many challenges facing us at Alina Lodge. The student population had dropped below 30; morale had dropped with it; staff had been downsized; and there were the corresponding financial losses that, at so many treatment centers, had threatened or closed them. A decimation had occurred and been caused, in many cases, by "managed care" rulings, and lack of appropriate benefits for treatment. Even at 90 years of age, Mrs Delaney had provided a legacy which furnished a strong foundation in the storm. Her fund-raising abilities, not known by many, had produced debt free facilities and property. They had left an endowment that would anchor our turnaround. There was further strength in the fact that we also were a self-pay facility; for Mrs. D. had believed (since the late 1980's) that insurance benefit dependency posed a real threat to the clinical integrity of addiction recovery programs.

I had some special opportunities at the beginning. I lived with the students for a week, which some thought a little odd for a new CEO; but that proved to be a very enlightening experience. I also spent a good deal of time with Mrs. Delaney over the ensuing five months in an experience I will cherish forever. I felt like a ball player must feel on joining the Yankees and still having "Babe Ruth" in the dugout. But Mrs. Delaney's mentoring was invaluable. We had known each other for years. She was one of my heroes in the field. Just to be welcomed and approved by her was an incredible gift. Lots more of my program education came from asking, listening to, and intently observing veteran staff, trustees, alumni, family members, students, referents, and professional colleagues.

The Lodge program is simple in its basic philosophy. However, there is much structure and detail, and there are many consequences, nuances, and strategies. These are complex to absorb. They are a challenge to manage. You can see from this book that there was astute, sound, reasoning behind the effectiveness of the program. In many ways, taking over leadership was easy for me. I had loved the program and made referrals to it (with good results) for the previous twenty years! Among my peers, I was considered a real "old school," Big Book, 12 Step philosophy guy with some modern clinical training that enhanced the basics of AA's spiritual program of recovery. This background fit in well with Lodge culture and philosophy. The program had clinical integrity. It had roots of the best in 12 Step, God-centered philosophy. And, it presented a dream come true for me personally as well as professionally. In fact, my professional mentor for many years was a Lodge alumnus (Dr. Robert S.), who had become a foremost recovering psychiatrist and program director in the addiction profession. There was great excitement for me.

This job would offer to me a tremendous chance to preserve the Delaney legacy *and* to bring the Lodge back to national prominence as a unique program and resource for the "reluctant to recover"–for students from all over the U.S. and the world.

Having a strong belief in your mission and having confidence in the effectiveness of clinical services provided are both essential ingredients in offering a community relations message that will increase utilization or student census. I believed in the Alina mission and had confidence in the program's effectiveness. Coupled with the legendary reputation and record of achievement by the Lodge under Mrs. Delaney, our team could and should be more than able to effectuate our business turnaround and our climb back into the national marketplace. In fact, I felt sure we could compete with anyone and be of service to all providers given our specialty with difficult cases. *Mission and service, the real backbone of the Little Hill-Alina Lodge, would continue to be our driving force and main focus for insuring our future.*

Geraldine Delaney had fashioned a brilliant program whose effectiveness with difficult cases was renowned. Continuous evaluation, calculated innovation, and fearless commitment to instincts and professional beliefs about recovery were Mrs. D.'s hallmarks. They could, when necessary, and even after her passing, be called upon to enable a critical yet controversial amendment in Lodge policy. There was, I felt, a very controversial amendment to long-standing lodge policy, and Mrs. D.'s heartfelt beliefs, that needed to be confronted, accepted, and adopted.

The treatment of alcohol and drug addicted clients with dual disorders (who needed medicine and modern psychopharmocological management by a psychiatrist) were not permitted as part of the Lodge program when I arrived. As this book makes clear, Mrs. Delaney had a strong bias against students' taking *any* medication, especially mood altering drugs. On that point, she was a firm. That such drug-consumption was dangerous was Mrs. Delaney's strongly held belief conviction–one born, in part, of the personal experience with her beloved husband, Tom Delaney. She had held her ground despite major breakthroughs in the quality of psychotropic, "mood stabilizing" medicines that were not mood changing or subject to abuse or sale in the streets. Alina Lodge stood solid on this policy long after other major centers such as Hazelden, Betty Ford, and Father Martin's had gone through an evolution. I believed that the Lodge's inability and reluctance to admit, evaluate, and treat those types of clients was hurting the Lodge. Hurting it in the professional community; severely restricting its ability to treat a wider range of clients with primary substance abuse addiction; and–most importantly–preventing the Little Hill Foundation from fulfilling its mission of treating the most difficult, chronic, treatment resistant, "reluctant to recover" cases of addiction.

The Executive Committee of the Board of Trustees showed wisdom, flexibility, and courage in its willingness to consider this major, much-needed, proposed change. I stated very clearly during the recruitment process that I was uncomfortable with any discrimination toward addicts with co-existing disorders. I said and felt strongly that this policy would need to be changed if the Lodge were to be successful in the 21st century. The Board approved the basic change I felt was so necessary.

Upon my hiring, we set we were able to define and pursue four key goals that would insure our future: (1) Preserve the legacy, philosophy, and program of long-term addiction recovery that is the cornerstone of our mission; (2) Treat a wider range of addicted clients and add the necessary adjunct clinical components to the main program–more effectively to treat the students and help prevent relapse via their co-existing disorders. (3) Launch a public relations and referral development campaign that would: (a) enable a more customer-friendly admission process; (b) re-establish our referral sources and educate them as to our expanded capabilities; (c) launch a professional public relations and marketing campaign--regionally and nationally--that would re-establish us as a quality provider and vital resource link in the national system of treatment services; and (4) Create a state-of- the- art fund-raising and development system and capability that would provide financial security for the foundation and protect our low cost/long term addiction treatment mission into the 21st century.

Challenges and Progress Made

Goal 1: Preserving the legacy, philosophy, and program

It is never easy to follow a legendary founder or to "fill those shoes." Mrs. Delaney–along with other well-known successful personalities–often recognized and stated something like, "It will take five people to replace me." This idea might well have represented an accurate assessment of, and tribute to, Geraldine Delaney's incredible personal and professional abilities. And her surviving staff, trustees, and alumni remained loyal and dedicated to the mission that had saved their own lives and accomplished the miracles they had watched every day at the Lodge. For me, then, it was to be an honor and a privilege to lead our team in preserving this program. To do less would not have been wise, nor could it have happened among the ranks of an army of "true believers" harboring 40 years of gratitude. You could never replace Geraldine Delaney personally. However, our teams can work, and are working together and using "group power" to keep the essence of program and legacy moving forward. In a word, our primary goal of preservation has been successful to this very date.

A legacy of philosophy, program, principles, rules, structure, policies, and procedures enables an organization and group of individuals to learn, train, adopt, follow, and implement a consistent way of thinking. Also, to deliver a set of services where consistency and unity of purpose can continue to flourish. Though often born of founders, entrepreneurs, and visionary leaders, such qualities-- seemingly reserved by God to the very few--can nonetheless be carried on by individuals and groups who may not themselves have such capabilities. I liken our situation to that in A.A. itself where there could be and was growth and success despite the decline and loss of its founders' influences. The traditions and heritage of the Lodge were powerful. They could be carried forth by seasoned staff and veterans whose instincts and knowledge had become part of their own experience and intuition.

In sum, then, we could not only manage and preserve the strength of the legacy, philosophy and long-term recovery program; but such management and preservation were essential to continuing our success. The basic engine that drives our mission *would* stay in place. Our tradition of innovation would now also be called upon to effectuate our second goal.

Goal 2: Treating a wider range of students with disorders co-existent with their primary addiction

We were blessed and fortunate to recruit and hire a Lodge alumna, Dr. Joyce B., as our Director of Psychiatry. She had achieved over 25 years of recovery and over 20 as an Addiction Specialist (ASAM Certified). She had invaluable knowledge of the Lodge, addiction treatment, and management of coexisting disorders. Also, as to staff training. These capabilities proved of immense value to our program to add adjunct clinical components.

One of our attending physicians, Dr. Joe C., an addiction specialist for many years, agreed to become our Medical Director, further ensuring our addiction-based service delivery capacity. Also, Dr. Lou Schlesinger, a nationally recognized psychologist with over twenty-five years addiction experience, joined our staff as a consultant. With specially designed testing batteries and evaluations, he helps diagnose significant personality disorders and major organic, memory, learning capacity issues to help focus treatment plans and progress in rehabilitation ability. Accompanied by my own clinical supervision experience, this very experienced and capable team of doctors, along with our seasoned Lodge staff, provided the leadership needed for success with our new clinical capacity.

Staff education and training were themselves another critical component. We must commend the "Delaney seasoned" and veteran clinical and nursing staff of the Lodge for their willingness, flexibility, and "quick study" of our new clinical services. These people were eager and excited to learn new skills; and they also were unusually effective mentors to the new staff in educating them as to Lodge philosophy and traditions.

Finally, some specialty groups were added to an already busy student schedule. Several in the series of lectures were converted to relapse prevention and codependency workshops. Consultant specialists were added to work with concomitant eating disorders as well as trauma survivors. All specialty groups are separate for men and women and designed to help prevent relapse in recovery. Only those students may attend who have been referred, when they are ready, by the treatment team.

These adjunct groups are designed to include students with dual disorders requiring medicine, and students with serious personality disorders. Also, students with eating disorders; students requiring trauma (sexual & other) services; students with unresolved grief, severe shame, and feelings impairment; and those with gambling addiction. These relapse prevention groups may add a few hours of programming to a student's work. However, they still do and must remain focused on spiritual recovery. The groups do not let sympathy or "manipulating use" of disability, relieve students from their responsibilities and from applying 12 Step recovery principles to complete the traditional program. This is a key focus that staff and students must keep in mind. Therefore eighty-five to ninety percent of the traditional programming for addiction recovery, as well as the disciplined spiritual design for living, remain the cornerstone of the treatment program.

We are succeeding in our second goal as well. We have successfully admitted many students who heretofore would not have been able to utilize our services. They are in recovery and doing "terrific." Many students have come here on psychiatric medicines from the myriad of new "stabilization programs" and "mental health systems" now treating addiction. Often such students have been "misdiagnosed." The Lodge carefully withdraws such students from these medicines when appropriate.

As managed care decimated the addiction treatment system in America, some of the "quick fix," "microwave," addiction recovery systems have overused anti-depressants. Those systems have taken us back 20 years to the confusion over early primary depression versus depressive symptoms caused by substance abuse and addiction. Our

Lodge has tremendous advantages in clearing up these important clinical issues. The advantages exist because of the long-term stays, "tincture of time" ability to evaluate and observe, and a change of focus based on the behavioral realities–all available because of the nature of our Lodge programming.

Overall, we have become a top quality, cost-effective provider of dual disorder services. These services–when coupled with the longer term, tincture of time, no-nonsense, no distraction, non-permissive approach–have been "life savers" for many dual disorder addiction clients. Often, such clients have sadly and unsuccessfully been shuffled between mental health and addiction care providers. Again, it cannot be verbalized enough that primary addiction recovery through 12 Step based treatment strategies must remain the key focus if students are to receive lasting sobriety that will allow them also to recover from other, co-existing disorder issues which may also face them in their recovery.

Goal 3: Developing public relations and referral campaigns relying on our mission and legacy as central themes for re-entry into the national marketplace

When I joined the Lodge, our services were still sorely needed by so many, and our mission and legacy were vital; but a decade of dormant referral development had to be overcome and quickly! Managed care had decimated 30 day treatment centers and thereby severely diminished the Lodge referral base. At the same time, the extended, longer term care end of the business had been in a growth mode. And we found that our competition in the longer term, self-pay market was greater than it ever had been since the Lodge began.

Fortunately, I had a successful and comprehensive background in national marketing campaigns. Perhaps like a "younger Mrs. Delaney," I also knew many of the key leaders, administrators and referral sources in the treatment industry. But there was another factor to be dealt with. Mrs. Delaney had done all the public relations and referral development herself. She had mainly relied on her successful results, reputation, sober alumni, word of mouth and effective treatment; and all had produced several decades of "full with a waiting list" success. However, there had been a decade of decline in Mrs. Delaney's activity. Our student census was at 30, down from over 80 in the peak years. This was a setting which needed immediate rectification.

To the Lodge's credit, three very key adjunct tools for marketing were started by the Board just prior to my arrival. These involved a booth to attend conferences; a video of the Lodge; and a book about Mrs. Delaney and Alina Lodge (this book). I was particularly excited about the book because, for both old and new referral sources, it would provide an important link to our legacy and mission. The book would also preserve and underline the Lodge's legendary toughness, effective results, and well respected founder.

On a shoe string budget, we traveled to key conferences and marketplaces throughout the country personally to build new, and to renew old, relationships for the Lodge. Our longtime Admissions Director, Jacki M., an alumna, was also very instrumental in this process. Later on, we hired Terry C. as our first community relations representative mainly to cover the Eastern Seaboard.

Our reentry into the national marketplace has gone very well. Our program additions and more "customer friendly" admissions policies were welcomed by referral sources. Our ability to work with a wider range of students and to offer expanded clinical capacity have been very well received by the professional community. Many older referral sources (including several treatment centers) have begun to reuse the Lodge. Also, we have many new referral sources. The results of this campaign speak for themselves. We were full to capacity again within a year after our programs were renewed. We have had to run a waiting list on several occasions. We are currently in the process of getting re-licensed additional beds (that already exist.) This will give us a capacity equal to that in the best years at the Lodge.

However, as established by Mrs. Delaney herself, our main focus in any public relations campaign must and will remain the effective results of long-term sobriety for the "reluctant to recover" that still enter the Lodge. This "sustained recovery goal" of our foundation's mission must always remain our focus. And we will continue to have a word-of-mouth, results oriented, reputation as the key to our success in the national group of addiction treatment providers.

Goal 4: Creating a state-of-the-art fund-raising system and capability to provide financial security for our foundation and protect our low cost, long term addiction treatment mission

Legendary founders like Mrs. D frequently design and develop successful systems for operations or fund-raising that are geared to their own unique strengths, style, work schedules, and innovative ways. Mrs. Delaney was a very successful and prolific fund raiser over her forty plus years. In fact, she raised millions of dollars for the Little Hill Foundation which operates Little Hill-Alina Lodge. She was keenly aware that, to protect the integrity of her long-term, low cost clinical mission, she would always have to keep her student fees low. She also knew some students would need additional funding to complete their program since their own family resources might run out before they were sufficiently healed.

With these key factors very clear, she quickly realized that all major building funds, capital funds, endowment funds (for interest income), off campus student residences, property, and so forth would have to be raised through philanthropy and by the operating margin of a business designed at best to break even. Also, to insure the clinical integrity of the mission, a scholarship fund, the G.O.D. (Geraldine Owen Delaney) Scholarship fund was established.

"I always raised the cash first before I built, bought or expanded anything. I never wanted to be in debt. You can make bad decisions when you are in debt," proclaimed Mrs. D. This very wise business principle ultimately saved the Lodge from going under as the "managed care storms" of the nineties put so many providers out of business. Despite the Lodge's decline in operating revenues, the debt free facilities and property, coupled with an endowment of reserve funds, kept the Lodge afloat until our current turnaround brought the operation back into the black.

Incredibly, Mrs. D. had raised most of this money herself–and mostly through grateful alumni, their families, friends and other associated benefactors. She would not let the Board of Trustees do fund-raising, although those that were able could, and did, give gifts and help make connections for further gifts. The whole fund-raising system relied on Mrs. D, her connections, her friends, alumni, her personal letter writing, her 3 x 5 index card system, her energy, and personal appearances throughout the country. This personal system, combined with an annual appeal ("the green envelope" that went out every year with the newsletter) around Thanksgiving time, was the only business plan and operation for the foundation.

Unfortunately, this highly "Mrs. D. dependent," personalized, fund-raising system–relying upon either difficult or non-existent records and with limited board or key staff involvement–began to slow down drastically. It stopped during the decade of the nineties. Mrs. D. herself slowed down as she reached her "eighties." She did not take as many trips; did not keep sufficient system records; outlived many of her friends, colleagues and contemporaries; and did not replace her personal system with people and systems that could carry on the vital funding for the preservation of the Lodge's mission. The whole system began to lose momentum and effectiveness.

Vitally needed funds for physical plant renovations and upgrades, future projects, endowment rebuilding, scholarship funding, and overall financial strength did not come in at a sufficient level over this decade. Moreover, there was no set system or program operated by qualified staff (unlike the clinical program, which *was*) into which one could step, manage, and keep in operation and thereby achieve needed goals.

Immediate remedial action was much needed. We (management, staff, and Trustees) collaborated and designed a strategic plan for the 21st century. A Director of Development was recruited and hired; and we began establishing a state-of-the-art fund-raising system to provide vitally needed capital, endowment and scholarship funding. We are also developing initiatives to include Trustees in this capital fund-raising process and improve our overall philanthropic capabilities. The Executive Director now, and in future years to come, will still be very much included and in the center of this process, just as Mrs. D. was. However, in this century, with the great competition for funds, the higher costs of projects, and the continued difficulty and stigma involved in raising funds for addiction treatment, a stronger, more comprehensive system must be designed. A system that will include professionals, key staff, consultants, volunteers, alumni, and selectively recruited trustees who will lead and succeed in the enormous tasks that lie ahead. Our system will never again become dependent on any one individual. Instead, it will use a professional, select team approach to insure our foundation's future. Alumni will remain a key component, but not as exclusively as in the past.

In 1999, we launched a ten million dollar capital, endowment and scholarship campaign to renew and preserve our facilities, replenish our endowment for keeping costs low, and rebuild our "GOD" Scholarship Fund. These will maintain, in the 21st Century, our tradition of quality, effective, long-term treatment for recovery from addiction.

We are making progress on these plans, but the "tincture of time" will be involved in growing to our new levels of expectations and needs for the Lodge. The plans remain a high priority, as the very essence of our foundation's mission is dependent on our commitment and success in operating a successful not-for-profit foundation. One that preserves our clinical mission through our philanthropic pursuits and through meeting our fund-raising objectives. We welcome all who can and will, in joining us in our mission and preserving a very valuable national treatment resource for those afflicted with the disease of addiction.

8

The Lodge's Mission and "A Vision for You"

By Mark Schottinger, M.A.,
Executive Director of Alina Lodge

[As Bill Wilson completed drafting, and then wrote, the final chapter of the First Edition of A.A.'s Big Book, he called that chapter "A Vision For You." Wilson said:

> It may seem incredible that these men are to become happy, respected, and useful once more. How can they rise out of such misery, bad repute and hopelessness. The practical answer is that since these things have happened among us, they can happen with you. Should you wish them above all else, and be willing to make use of our experience, we are sure they will come. The age of miracles is still with us. Our own recovery proves that!

> Our hope is that when this chip of a book is launched on the world tide of alcoholism, defeated drinkers will seize upon it, to follow its suggestions. Many, we are sure, will rise to their feet and march on. They will approach still other sick ones and Fellowships of Alcoholics Anonymous may spring up in each city and hamlet, havens for those who must find a way out.

With a similar burst of optimism, determination, and confidence, Alina Lodge's new director wrote most of this chapter and used, as part of its title, "a vision for you." Most of the words are those of Mark Schottinger.]

The first printing of this book occurred at one of the most critical crossroads in the history of Alina Lodge. The whole treatment industry was and is still emerging from the ravages of a financial "rationing" system for behavioral health/addiction resource dollars. That system has been cloaked eloquently in the guise of "managed care." Yet it really refers to "managed costs." Given these challenges and problems, would and could the mission of the Lodge survive not only its own commitment to the highest standards of clinical integrity but also the crisis in the U.S. addiction treatment system. Fortunately, with great gratitude to God and to Mrs. Delaney, our staff, and trustees, we answer with a resounding, "Yes." In fact, in this environment we are needed more than ever.

First, we should ask: What then are the timeless and often unique strategies and principles of treatment that are the essence of Alina Lodge. We see them as follows:

- **Consistent with the early AA way, God and time** are definitely the major components of the recovery process at the Lodge; and they will remain as a cornerstone of the program.

- **Divine help, not merely self-help or therapeutic/medical help**, is an essential principle. Spirituality--reliance upon the power and presence of God--remains the underlying cornerstone of all rehabilitation strategies at the Lodge. This spiritual principle must stand as a priority above, but in conjunction with, any and all medical, clinical, or therapeutic, interventions and protocols. Standing on this power of God as A.A.'s primary solution, Bill Wilson quoted a staff physician at a world-renowned hospital who said: "[T]here is no doubt in my mind that you were 100% hopeless apart from Divine help" (Big Book of Alcoholics Anonymous, 1st ed., pp. 54-55). Wilson added: "We never apologize to anyone for depending upon our Creator. We can laugh at those who think spirituality the way of weakness. Paradoxically, it is the way of strength. The verdict of the ages is that faith means courage. All men of faith have courage. They trust their God. We never apologize for God. Instead we let Him demonstrate, through us, what He can do" (Big Book, 1st ed., p. 81).

- **"Tincture of Time"** remains a guiding force that recognizes the realities and ravages of addiction in chronic relapse, treatment resistant, "reluctant to recover" students. It can take many months just for the body and mind to "detoxify," for the brain fog to lift, for the feelings and emotional freeze to thaw, and for the student to *demonstrate* recovery ("walk the walk vs. just talk the talk") and build a disciplined design for living that works.

- **"Indeterminate length of stay"** is a simple but important concept that basically gives a powerful mandate to, and unique ability for rehabilitation at, the Lodge. Simply put, it means: When you are well enough to leave, we will let you go. That means you will have done the necessary work, demonstrated recovery principles in your actions and thinking, and are safe enough to go on to the next level of care or to be discharged to home. The indeterminate period means there must there be disease "symptom" relief and that body, mind and spirit must be healed enough to be reintegrated and functioning from the fragmentation of addiction. Further, demonstrated recovery must be evidenced on a consistent, sustained basis in behavior, actions, reactions, emotional response, critical thinking, and written assignments to verify actual vs. intended or verbal progress. This indeterminate length of stay is a very powerful and daily intervention tool. It combats the "self will run riot", ego-centricity, grandiosity, and often "feigned compliance" that our "treatment wise" students bring with them. In short, it provides daily ego deflation in depth, and it defeats manipulative attempts involving false surrender and compliance meant just to "do their time and leave." Students have to get well enough by our standards, not theirs, in order to be discharged.

- **The "non-permissive approach"** goes right back to a philosophy in the A.A. of earlier years. In those times, Dr. Harry Tiebout (an early friend and supportive psychiatrist of the fellowship) stated very clearly, "Surrender without a sustaining discipline to maintain that surrender and new life is useless." Alcoholics and addicts become very impulsive, impatient, dishonest, and self-seeking/self-centered. They begin making poor decisions, are extremely willful, have defense-driven denial about reality, are manipulative, and want to be judged on their intentions vs. their behaviors and actions. The Lodge combines discipline, structure, sleep/dietary requirements, communication policies (no phones, limited visitation, non-fraternization, the "write-it" system), extensive rules, codes of conduct, sanctions, and consequences. All are designed to counteract the foregoing addictive lifestyle characteristics. The system demands that "students" begin to live along spiritual lines. Overall, the "non-permissive approach" becomes another lifesaving support to prevent relapse and sustain recovery in the real world. When all is said and done, our students have lived and learned (for an extended period of time) the skills and structure necessary for living along spiritual lines. The tough discipline sustains their surrender and continuation in working their Steps and program when they depart from our staff and structure, and turn to A.A. support.

- **Family Care** is, and will remain, an essential component of the recovery process. Geraldine Delaney said many times: "The families can undo in five minutes what it has taken us five months to accomplish." The Lodge is often involved in well-financed enabling systems for students, special interventions, contracting, and other individualized clinical strategies for student and family members and significant others. These are fine crafted along with the classic 12 Step/Al-Anon philosophy of ongoing support. Longer care time permits many meetings and, when necessary, interventions over a long course of treatment. These enable evaluation of addiction dynamics and intervention that will end "deadly enabling," "entitlement," and "toxic shame" dynamics that can sabotage recovery and keep the elusive relapse cycle intact. Our in-residence abilities and in-depth staff expertise provide a lifesaving force for both students and family members. Alina Lodge provided one of the first in-residence family programs in the U.S., and our emphasis on treating the whole family through 12 Step spiritual recovery is one of our age old and most valued traditions!

• **AA Philosophy, 12 Steps, and the Big Book** shall forever remain at the core of the teachings and philosophy of Alina Lodge. Students must actually take the first eight Steps before leaving the Lodge. They must also endeavor to practice many of the principles inherent in Steps 9 - 12 while they are in treatment. 10th and 11th Step work is particularly important for learning daily spirituality, conscious contact with God, and God's own lifesaving discipline of the alcoholic/addict mentality and lifestyle. Study, sessions, lectures, assignments, guest lecturers, Big Book study, demonstration AA meetings, outside meetings, recovering guest lecturers and alumni, all provide a comprehensive education on this way of life. The Lodge is always disturbed to see how little of this essential 12 Step way of life and recovery has been understood and/or practiced by students despite numerous previous rehab stays. Such trends in seemingly superficial and token attention to spiritual recovery, the Big Book and the 12 Steps, will, and must, be changed when a student comes to Alina Lodge.

Quick fix, mental health strategies prove "powerless" over serious addiction. Student work must be focused on the use of our philosophy, their design for living, and fellowship step strategies if recovery in the real world is to be maintained. Alina Lodge graduates become very good and active members of the fellowship after their stay with us.

•   **Long-Term Treatment vs. "Detox/Stabilization", "28 day" and/or "Extended Care" Programs**. As we've said, there has been a managed care/insurance assault on addiction treatment. There has also been a twenty year regression in thinking and the treatment of addiction–a *regression* to mental health-"underlying symptom" approaches. The Lodge must therefore be very careful and discriminating in choosing the type of treatment, treatment philosophy, and emphasis among those being delivered in the clinical services of various programs throughout the U.S. Unfortunately today, cost containment objectives and financially-prejudiced treatment preferences so dominate the arena that most (approximately eighty-five percent) insurance plans and managed care firms will only allow a short combination of detox and stabilization with under 14 days of in-patient care.

Other well-known (and sometimes pricey) programs–often with a 60% or more self pay mix–still offer 28 day rehab. For some patients this is enough care. Yet even in these centers, severity of mental health or dual disorder symptoms become the primary justification for allowing further in-patient stays with 3rd party payers. The permitted stay is not based on the level of response to recovery and rehabilitation from addiction goals and 12 Step programming. These better run, addiction-focused, programs are still an oasis in the storm and can be successful with many cases. However, other cases still need much more time than detox and/or 28 days offer. In the decade of the nineties, many more self-pay, "extended care," phased type programs emerged with a usually three phase, 90 day program model. This type program can also be beneficial by providing a much longer time period in a protected environment.

Whereas "extended care" provides only partial treatment and sober living while the client is working and doing other activities, long-term treatment provides all-day, all evening, intensive treatment. The step down to less intensive treatment and less restrictive monitoring and behavioral management often comes immediately following a 28 day phase. Within 60 days, a client can be out all day working or in other activities–without full-time treatment. Again, for many cases, this can be sufficient and give added "protected environment" time to allow rehabilitation and recovery attitudes and behaviors to develop and strengthen.

The Lodge has been very blessed by the fact that many of the top programs throughout the United States do identify, intervene on, and refer to Alina some of the clients ascertained to need long-term treatment! Long-term treatment, especially as we define it at Alina Lodge, is just that. It means a continuation of intensive daily treatment for many months (indeterminate length of stay) without a set time limit or phases, but driven by the healing and progress of each individual. Further, the Lodge itself sometimes sends some of our students for additional time treatment at extended care type programs and very structured halfway houses. This after many months of long-term treatment at the Lodge. For very difficult, reluctant to recover, chronic relapse cases, long-term treatment is necessary for breaking strong, ingrained, thinking, behavior, and feeling patterns while providing the tincture of time for overall physical, mental, and emotional healing to occur. We have a 90 day minimum stay with an average between 5 to 7 months of care. Such long-term treatment as defined by Lodge standards is vastly, different from stabilization, 28 day, or extended care programs–many of which often claim to specialize in chronic relapse cases. However, the Lodge's programmatic, non-permissive/behavioral, spiritual, 12 Step emphasis, along with other programming features, is much more intense and, in fact, different from most other programs operating in today's field.

Alina believes firmly there is a lot more than meets the eye or the industry buzz words when one finally enters the place where hope can become fact.

- **"Student" vs. patient terminology** assures a very important conceptual difference in care at Alina Lodge. Mrs. Delaney often said: "I didn't send you an engraved invitation to come here. You needed to be here so you will respect our rules and our ways." We emphasize the *student* idea and word so clients know the staff isn't there to "fix them." Staff is there to help guide them in learning their new way of life as "students." To learn as students, they need to take responsibility for this learning process through written work and assignments. They need to learn proper behavior and become accountable for their behavior and not merely their intentions. Again, students were not invited but came with a critical need, and they must respect the rules and guidelines of the Lodge. Students are not at the Lodge to be "fixed" by doctors and therapists doing classic medical delivery; they need to demonstrate through their actions the walk versus the talk. The Lodge has many unique and effective ways within the myriad program components and structure that enable progress in rehabilitation to be observed and evaluated. To graduate with a key chain, a student must pass many "tests and standards" of internalized and externalized recovery in order to be discharged with staff approval.

- **Long term treatment via self-pay** has been one of the most courageous and visionary critical decisions that Mrs. Delaney and the Board were to make. This, as she knew, was the only way to protect the clinical integrity of the program and therefore the very essence of our mission, the best recovery opportunity for each individual student. She knew and challenged the threat that "insurance benefit dependency" held for addiction providers. She would not let insurance carriers and their "hired gun" managed care agents run the Lodge, her programs, her beloved students or the real needed course of their clinical care. Thank you, Mrs. D., for your courage, fearless commitment, and faith! The early warning signs of "managed care" in the eighties were smoked out and exposed by Mrs. D as a dangerous trend in substituting cost containment priorities over clinical integrity and in victimizing patients and their families by false and dishonest play on words and lives! Each potential client brings a unique history, level of damage/impairment, learning capability, and other qualities. Therefore, each person's healing ability and progress will be at his demonstrable rate and progress–one not pre-determined by accountants and lawyers who establish absolute minimum standards of care for cost containment purposes. A different focus and collaborative alignment toward long-term recovery is possible: Take away all financial incentives. Eliminate all adversaries. Utilize individual/family resources because there is family-tie motivation to preserve the life of a loved one. Make ultimate health, long-term relapse prevention, and recovery the mission.

Sadly, this type of treatment and mission is impossible to get funded by roughly ninety percent of the insurance carriers and "managed care" firms today. Moreover, and unfortunately, many Americans do not have and cannot find resources needed for a self-pay route. There is therefore intact today a health care rationing system that shows extreme prejudice against providing resources for long term addiction recovery. Fortunately the Lodge can and will bypass these trends. It can and will keep its clinical integrity and mission intact and do so via low cost, long term, self pay strategies.

- **Non-fraternization Policy**—Men and women are not allowed to "fraternize" at the Lodge. Talking, looking, passing notes to each other, and other fraternizing may result in discharge. Designed to avoid any type of emotional and/or physical relationships between men and women, this policy makes a clear and serious statement about recovery, dependence, and choice. Students may choose to rely on God and recover, or to rely on male-female emotional relationship dependency or other assorted monkey business distractions. Separate dining tables, lecture seating, group work, residences, strict rules, walking tracks, programming, and female primary case managers help preserve this important tradition. The tradition also helps build discipline since student men and student women are on same campus and in same large halls and not totally separated. This separated but not isolated policy requires the daily discipline in a reality setting, rather than an out-of-sight, out-of-mind type experiment. Students are then better prepared to deal with the temptations and to rely on the discipline the real world will require! This policy also recognizes very strongly that men and women are different and have gender specific as well as other important needs in a recovery process that can be individualized and served in the Lodge model.

• **Minimizing distractions and limiting communication**—Family members are often thrilled to learn that Lodge students cannot use the telephone (except for emergency or legal issues under staff supervision); that visitation is limited and corresponds to therapeutic progress; and that a casual rehab array of pools, gyms, tennis courts, recreational programs, and off- grounds passes are not part of Lodge philosophy and programming. There is to be no distraction from the primary recovery mission. The discipline is designed to help foster a steady "mirroring" and focus on one's life, character defects, and recovery process instead of a "defocus" on the recovery process and focus on the distractions, recreation, excessive exercise, play, entertainment, and other diversions many are so used to doing during rehabilitation. And doing as a substitute for meeting their real needs and work.

Always ready with a quip to support her policies, Mrs. Delaney proclaimed to students: "You didn't come here to learn how to recreate, I think you're pretty good at doing that already." On the other hand, students can have healthy exercise through daily walking on specific tracks and with certified instructors conducting aerobic exercise classes two to three times each week to help with physical recovery.

The Lodge prefers communication with family and friends (on a pre-approved consent list) by written letters. Also students must ask for solutions to many of their wants and needs through the Lodge's famous "green write it" system. The "write-its" are then submitted to staff. Students are forced to improve their thinking process and judgment; slow down their impulsiveness; take a written look at "entitlements," narcissism , and self-centered processes; slow down for making better decisions; improve their frustration tolerance level; and be prevented from imposing, interrupting, and bypassing rules and procedures just to satisfy their every whim and emotional discharge. There is a belief they are also thereby encouraged to seek both staff and student peer advice in their communications with others so they can improve their overall honesty, integrity, and unselfish concern for the needs of others.

This critical recovery process occurs on a daily basis at the Lodge with numerous other rules and procedures that chip away at ego, self-will run riot, self-centeredness, impulsive bad decisions, and non-spiritual behavior classically regarded as addiction "character defects."

- **Diet/Nutrition, Sleep, Sugar/Junk Food, Caffeine/Nicotine and Exercise**—A key component of the Lodge's non-permissive, structured approach to learning a new way of life integrates the basic hierarchical survival needs of food, shelter, rest and healthy living habits into daily Lodge guidelines and rules. Geraldine Delaney had a professional background in both nutritional programming and in the medical-healthcare field, prior to achieving her own sobriety and founding the Lodge. Mrs. Delaney placed great importance on healthy habits in nutrition and daily living. A very healthy, balanced, high protein, low carbohydrate diet of nutritious meals has been an important dietary tradition at Alina Lodge. One small dessert per day at dinner (often just fresh fruit) is all the sugar that is allowed. No candy, soda, sugar filled junk food, caffeine, or other poor nutritional items are allowed. The usual array of candy, junk food, and soda machines are nowhere to be found on Lodge property. No caffeinated drinks of any kind are allowed.

Another visionary and very courageous change that Mrs. Delaney implemented in 1985 (thereby becoming the first rehab in the U.S. to do so), was to ban the possession and smoking of all nicotine products on Lodge property. Her belief in the addictive and destructive nature of nicotine motivated a change and resolve that many others have tried and failed at. To this day, the ban still holds at the Lodge. No smoking of any kind is allowed on property (by staff, students, contractors or delivery persons). Students are offered a patch to help with withdrawal from nicotine, and classes on nicotine dependence are part of Lodge programming.

Sleep is also regulated, in that students must be in bed, lights out, for eight hours each night whether they can or cannot sleep, whether they wake up early or not, and whether they want to or not. They are required to learn to take 8 hours of rest and be still. Exercise is encouraged through walking only on designated tracks (separate for men and women); and students now participate in an aerobics class with medical clearance, led by a certified instructor. No running, jogging, or physical sports are allowed.

All the foregoing healthy living components, rules and structure, of course, stand in marked contrast to the poor habits of sleep, diet, exercise, junk food, caffeine/nicotine that over 90% of all addicts have plummeted into. Many other rehabs are much more "permissive" in their approach and teachings in this area. Hence many of the poor lifestyle habits are allowed to continue even while "counseling rehabilitation" is taking place. The healthy lifestyle habits enforced during a stay at the Lodge help the student internalize and externalize a new discipline for right living that can be counted on, and carried forward, into the student's ongoing recovery The new habits serve as an element of relapse prevention as well.

- **Socialization, Dining, Codes of Conduct, Rules, Dress, and Behavior**—Restoring dignity, respect, discipline, structure, and proper behavior towards self and others is another major component of rehabilitation at Alina Lodge. There is to be a basic "golden rule" way of life, which means actually living along spiritual lines, walking the walk, not just talking the talk "How is your behavior today, according to whose standards?" was a constant greeting and refrain by Mrs. D. It has continued by the staff toward students. Peer group interaction, social skills level, attitudes, emotional intensity or lack thereof, ability to follow rules, general conduct, interaction and sensitivity toward others, levels of honesty, physical appearance, level of discipline, consistency of emotion and behavior over time, overall healing level, therapeutic participation, quality of completion of assignments, and many other qualities are all observed, evaluated and rehabilitated on a daily basis by the multi-disciplinary staff of the Lodge. Students must sit for an hour together at meals with jacket and tie and dresses for dinner. They must rotate tables, engage in no table cross talk, and comport themselves with proper conduct and manners. Such requisites illustrate a few of the many socialization/behavior techniques of the Lodge. Other rules and structures, too numerous to mention, are all designed to help foster a spiritual, disciplined and successful way of life in recovery. Students must live that way of life on a daily basis in actions and attitudes, not merely learn or talk about it. A real, live, human laboratory for recovery takes place with fish-bowl-like observation and evaluation to monitor progress and ensure comprehensive rehabilitation.

Sophisticated, treatment-wise compliance, denial, and slick dishonesty can be impacted, intervened on, and changed in such an environment. Somewhat enigmatically, Geraldine Delaney trumpeted: "The students have made all the rules here." Their tragedies, relapses, schemes, and an incredible program are all part of the process that guards against a cunning, baffling, and powerful disease. The daily, weekly, and monthly structured, non-permissive, behavioral approach to recovery at the Lodge provides a concise and solid foundation for long-term sobriety and relapse prevention.

- **Specialized in treating "The Reluctant to Recover"**—Geraldine Delaney coined the "reluctant to recover" term to describe the chronic relapse, treatment resistant, and very treatment wise students who find their way to Alina Lodge. Often leveraged and in serious trouble! The Lodge was once described on a national news show as "the last chance saloon for recovery" out in western New Jersey. Many professionals and family members throughout the U.S., as well as I myself, have always entertained hope for any difficult addiction cases if we could get them to Alina Lodge. This concentration of a reluctant, multiple failure, student population at the Lodge makes a very powerful, common-cause, easily identifiable, fellowship. Students quickly observe the desperation, fear, and sense of hopelessness which mark the similarities of their shared histories of failure in recovery. However, they also become galvanized and engaged in a unique bonding process that inspires a sense of hope and fellowship--often quite different from, and much deeper than, that found in their previous experiences. In short, they find a peer group, composed of those who have tried everything, and now must work harder than ever before. They often feel impelled to make this "last chance" program–so different and difficult–work for them to save their lives. There is a special combination of the Lodge's unique mission and lifesaving reputation, which is coupled with the motivation of a very difficult (but seemingly hopeless and spiritually bankrupt) group of students. The particular combination offers a renewed hope and belief in recovery. In fact, our mission's tag line is very appropriate and supportive for students and their families: We are "a place where hope can become fact."

- **"Affluenza," Entitlement, Power, and Position**—can be powerful forces, not only in fueling and enabling addiction to grow and worsen, but also as deadly in sabotaging the recovery process. Mrs. D. had a term she used when describing the difficulty many wealthy/entitled individuals had with recovery. She spoke of them as the "underprivileged rich", with the emphasis on underprivileged. In her book *The Golden Ghetto,"* Jacki O'Neil uses the term "affluenza" to describe some of the serious problems that wealth, privilege, and entitlement can cause in life, in addiction, and as a barrier to recovery. The symptoms can be many. But they do include: low self-esteem; grandiosity/arrogance; lack of trust; poor interpersonal boundaries; paid surrogate parenting; low frustration tolerance; narcissism; impulse control problems; enabling; and corruption/coercion to keep money, jobs or inheritance. Although these characteristics are common among many addicts, they can be more ingrained and disabling in more affluent backgrounds. Money, in and of itself, can be like a drug and a very powerful one. Money and power can also directly interfere with the real need for a relationship with God. They can therefore sabotage the very essence of recovery via spiritual principles and surrender to a power greater than one's self (rather than surrendering to money or power). Due to the nature of Alina's highly regarded program in circles throughout the U.S. (as well as our self-pay, low cost programming), we have treated many people of means. People who own their own businesses, have earned or inherited wealth, are professionals (doctors, lawyers, financiers, pilots, clergy), are managers, have trust funds, or hold positions in family businesses. Also, their relatives, spouses, children, grandchildren and colleagues. The financial, societal, and cultural levels of such students provide a like peer group at Alina Lodge, but the program itself provides a powerful solution and new way of living that can be a lifesaving antidote to affluenza, entitlement, money and power. We have served and will continue to serve this group of students in a comprehensive and effective manner.

- **Relapse Prevention and Coexisting Disorders**—"There are those, too, who suffer from grave emotional and mental disorders, but many of them do recover if they have the capacity to be honest." (Big Book, Chapter 5, How it Works). Like the general population, alcoholics and drug addicts can have other types of mental and emotional disorders, personality disorders, eating disorders, trauma history, and other addictions (work, sex, gambling, relationships, codependency, adrenaline/risk taking, food, compulsive spending, and others). Mrs. D had a general definition for addictions: "Addiction equals pain plus learned relief." But, and unfortunately, "coexisting disorders" which often accompany primary chemical dependency can cause relapse into alcohol/drug addiction if left untreated. There is another important side of the picture, however: Nothing can be treated or worked on unless the alcoholism/drug addiction is arrested and stabilized first. To quote from Sigmund Freud, "You can't help anyone if they are not present and available to be helped." When people lapse into active chemical addiction, they are not available to be helped.

The goal of abstinence from all mood changing drugs must be achieved and sustained to make progress in any other areas, including the major coexisting disorders. Tragically, professionals all over the U.S. and in the world do not yet understand this simple, basic principle; and they try, without avail, to treat "other issues" while the primary addiction rages on and blocks any and all progress. In order for dual disorder treatment to be successful, first and foremost, the alcohol/drug addiction needs to be treated, stabilized, and removed or "maintained" via 12 Step spiritual solution in the fellowship. With such an approach as a foundation, concurrent treatment strategies for coexisting disorders can be carefully integrated. Also, a good and accurate assessment/evaluation by seasoned professionals in addiction, can clearly identify other disorders and addictions. Then, if non-addictive, mood stabilizing medicine can actually help a psychiatric condition, competent, certified addiction doctors can manage that component. Further, if other addictions, personality disorders, or a myriad combination of coexisting disorders are present as well, competent, trained psychologists, therapists, counselors and other specialists can assess, provide, and deliver concurrent therapy and step work that can help alleviate and reduce the impact of these issues, especially in early recovery.

Overall, dual disorders are mainly treated behaviorally through 12 Step spiritual principles, just like the primary addiction. A practical and basic use of slogans, Steps, prayer, daily inventory, (followed by right action) offer a powerful combination that can be applied to coexisting disorders as well. However, 85 - 90% of the focus in rehabilitation *must* be on the primary addiction and the 12 Step solution. This enables maintenance of sobriety while other issues begin to heal. Yet it is equally important to understand that major coexisting disorders left undiagnosed and untreated can be a very significant trigger for relapse into alcoholism and drug addiction.

All these issues can be and are being treated successfully and cost-effectively at Alina Lodge–a program which therefore holds out a tremendous beacon of hope for those afflicted with dual disorders.

- **Alumni, Guest Lecturers, 12 Step Community**—There is
  a rewarding stream of alumni, guest lecturers, and sober AA
  members (often with many years of success) who share their
  experience, strength and hope with the students in a variety
  of programmatic components throughout a typical week.
  Also, Lodge alumni, who come back to celebrate
  anniversaries from all over the U.S., are a unique group who
  know full well the difficulty current students are going
  through and give much encouragement and hope. Their
  message: "Stay and get your key chain, and you will be
  profoundly grateful for the rest of your life." Alina Lodge is
  a tough rehab. And when an alumnus speaks, one is often
  reminded of a fairly common Marine Corps sentiment.
  Former Marines know the sacrifice required of recruits in
  order for them to graduate; yet the grads do not want to see
  one thing made one bit easier or different among the
  newcomers that follow. For the simple reason that lives are
  saved in battle by tough discipline in training.

Alina Lodge has a long history and roots going back to the very
beginning of A.A. when Geraldine Delaney was "12 Stepped" by her
brother, and by Bill Wilson, and Lois. There is therefore a strong
spiritual presence and A.A.-like tradition that still flourishes there.
And this attracts a seasoned and motivated crowd of recovering folks
(including many professionals) from all over. The students see and
hear a tremendous parade of recovering people from all walks of life
during a typical 6 - 8 month stay at the Lodge. A very motivated and
special lifetime comradery is also established through the work of
Lodge alumni with newly discharged students and family members.
We believe it is deeper and more far reaching than that which can be
established at many rehabs in this day and age. Students also develop
a lasting bond of support and friendship that continues with the staff
for years. Finally, students and family members share a unique and
close relationship arising out of the life-saving results of spending
unusual amounts of time together in rehab. The Alina Lodge loyalty
and friendship have produced grateful halfway houses, professionals,

AA groups, and sponsors. These have told us many times they love to get our students in aftercare because they are such "died in the wool" AA/spiritual members. Graduates' commitment to, enthusiasm for, and discipline in the program and fellowship are much noticed and much appreciated.

- **Dedicated Staff**—Mrs. D. developed a loyalty and commitment by her staff to Alina Lodge and its program that is rare in the work world today. Many grateful staff remain for decades. Workers share the conviction that Alina Lodge is a different and special place. Lodge people–from housekeeping through the Board of Trustees--believe in what we do. They provide dignity and show respect for each individual student and his or her family. This truly produces a big part of the hope for a life in recovery that the students begin to feel and internalize. Hope, dignity, respect, and confidence are powerful health restoratives; and students simply do not see our staff "blink" in their commitment to students, the Lodge, or their firm belief that recovery is possible.

Let's look at the bit of heaven on earth clinicians find in working at the Lodge. Some could never have imagined the possibility of working with a student until he or she is really healthy enough to leave and to move on to the next level. How unusual is our statement to students: "When you are well enough to go according to our standards of rehabilitation, you will be notified." Managed care, insurance companies, fixed lengths of stay, and financial issues are, most of the time, eliminated from the treatment course. Pure clinical considerations can then drive our rehabilitation plan. Often today an entity seems to provide a simple, logical, approach to health restoration. It may, as well, give lip-service to the approach. Rarely, however, can such an apparently simple, logical program deliver results with the clinical integrity to be found in Lodge programming.

A little bit of heaven, then, for the clinician and manager who finds a real opportunity at the Lodge, and with its program. For the

Lodge and its program enable a staff member to stick with a student until really desired results have been achieved.

But there's a challenge that goes with the opportunity. Some of the smartest, sickest, slickest, treatment-wise students in the world enter the Lodge with shattered hopes and extensive histories of relapse after previous, failed treatment attempts. Many arrive with various enabling systems intact and/or present in various forms of leveraged agenda: Threatened loss of professional licenses, actual job loss, an alternative to incarceration, a pending divorce, a transfer from jails or psych hospitals and detoxes, possible revocation of trust funds, loss of their businesses, life-threatening physical diseases which are symptoms of addiction. Students face long-term lengths of stay—with an average of six to eight months, and often much more. There is frequently a serious nature and progression of their chronic relapse history. These situations require a special breed of staff which can effectively handle such difficult cases. Still more challenges are frequent. Many students also have been in positions of power and prestige, are independent professionals, have serious and severe entitlement backgrounds, are often very wealthy with guaranteed incomes, and often have very complicated and toxic (to recovery) marriage and family systems. Lodge case managers have all been in recovery for many years themselves [The author prefers the A.A. expression "recovered," which is the watchword of A.A.'s Big Book, but is frequently anathema to professionals]. Long-term recovery or sobriety, then, and an average professional background of at least 10 - 15 years of experience (many 20 or more), is what a case manager offers.

Working with Alina cases is much more about the "art of counseling" than the "craft of counseling." To match the capability of their more seasoned counter-parts, even experienced counselors may have to spend at least six months to a year of work before they can become the effective and astute in the Lodge's programming. Students can often run over like a bus any staff with less experience in recovery and professional work. Training, orientation, and supervision of staff are vital requirements for Lodge success. And finding Lodge-caliber staff in the world of "quick fix," "microwave," mental-health-dominated treatment systems is an ongoing challenge for the Lodge as it holds fast to its principles and integrity in this 21st century.

- **Philanthropy, Clinical Integrity, G.O.D. Scholarship Fund, Astute Business Practices**—One of the key ingredients in the success of Mrs. Delaney's program at Alina Lodge was her "tincture of time" concept. We live in business worlds where time is money, and Mrs. D. was visionary in her understanding of the money versus time-needed dilemma presented to families and students entering the Lodge. Even for people of means, many months of our daily rate can add up. Our healing factor of "time" can only be applied if costs are kept low. And keeping costs low has to be in company with several business strategies that have major philanthropy and fund-raising as support for their effectuation.

Cost-containment practices at Alina meant: A no frills, nothing fancy, approach to treatment itself. A very practical and Spartan "lodge like" facility with paneling and linoleum instead of wallpaper and carpeting. Avoidance of elaborate recreational facilities which were not even desired. Simple, basic furnishings and appointments. A shoestring public relations budget without heavy marketing or advertising expense. Grooming your *own* staff to avoid facing premium priced hiring in the open marketplace. Establishing a very lean, unlayered, and "working foreman" type management staff. Keeping a tightfisted central purchasing system for all supplies. Acquiring in-kind donations from friends and alumni for construction projects, service contracts, equipment, furnishings, supplies, and so forth. And running a low-margin, break-even operation that enables minimization of costs to consumers. The counterpart of such business strategies is that they make the entity heavily dependent on philanthropy to support all capital projects, renovations, new construction, equipment, furnishings, and other items because the operating margin doesn't supply a profit sufficient to pay for them.

In addition to its unique cost-containment program, the Lodge created an endowment fund whose income could help meet the annual operating budget. This further enabled the Lodge to keep costs low. This endowment, wherever possible, also reduced or avoided annual rate increases to the end that inflation and high rates would not erode the essence of the mission: which was and is low cost, long-term, affordable treatment. As stated earlier, this endowment fund literally saved the Lodge from going under–consistent with another of its purposes, which was to cover a possible rainy day storm–something that really did hit in the mid nineties.

The Lodge has another fund, in addition to its endowment fund. It has been popular and has elicited many alumni contributions. It is called the G.O.D. (Geraldine Owen Delaney) Scholarship Fund; and it is primarily used for people who may run out of resources but still need more time and rehabilitation before they are ready to be discharged. In addition, a certain number of scholarships are given to needy students each year. Of course, the downside of all of this is that not everyone can afford to come to the Lodge. Potential clients must be screened very carefully during the pre-admission process to be sure their clinical stay will not be jeopardized by financial issues. As stated previously, some insurance carriers will contribute payments. But we leave this additional possibility for financial assistance wholly in the hands of the insurance carrier and the family. Doing so, the Lodge is not subjected to financial incentives or interference with a successful course of treatment.

All the afore-mentioned business practices and philanthropic strategies contribute to and protect the clinical integrity of Alina Lodge. Our foundation's mission--from the Board through all the staff--is to help provide the best possible quality care experience for each individual student and family in their recovery from alcoholism and drug addiction.

- **Educational Role and Industry Leadership**—If you travel around the United States, you can gain an understanding of the educational and leadership influence Mrs. Delaney and Alina Lodge have had on the addiction treatment field and on countless professionals. Mrs. D's profound and pioneering influence on many fronts includes: Mentorship; role modeling; original programmatic designs; visionary clinical insights and protocols for addiction; specialization in treatment (chronic relapse/long term); education and treatment for multiple professional groups; education presentations all over the U..S; alcoholism council start-ups; training of staff to enable the starting of new treatment centers; lecturing at the Rutgers Summer School, SECAD, and other international training venues; providing one of the earliest in residence family treatment programs in U.S.; being one of the original long-term, 12 Step treatment programs in U.S.; offering one of the first low cost/self-pay models; truly individualized care with indeterminate length of stay vs. set program time frames; having unusual and profound motivational/spiritual/fellowship relationships and bonds with AA members and communities around the U.S.; operating a very successful private, not-for-profit, philanthropic-business model in the treatment industry; protection and independence of the Lodge's clinical integrity from any and all influence by government funding and agencies, insurance companies, managed care firms, and third party programmatic regulations (JCAHO, CARF); a beacon of hope for all other professionals and treatment centers with difficult, reluctant to recover cases; an incredible "courage of conviction" and highly principled conductor of business and programming--both visionary and courageous; a tough, no-nonsense approach to addiction treatment that was also just as filled with compassion and hope ("love and service"–as characterized by A.A.'s Dr. Bob) matched by few; and an "unshakable faith" in God and the spiritual principles and Twelve Steps of A.A. as the true foundation of all recovery.

There are now many well known treatment centers, professionals, councils, innovative recovery systems, professional groups, and societies, addiction industry leaders, and of course, countless grateful individuals and their families who will tell you their histories of gratitude and success in which Mrs. Delaney and Alina Lodge played an integral part and provided leadership influence.

As we enter this 21st century, having survived the industry tragedies in addiction treatment integrity in the nineties, perhaps Alina Lodge can again provide a beacon of hope, offer a successful non-profit business model, and play an educational leadership role for the addiction treatment industry. Mrs. Delaney's heritage can again provide in the future an influence and mentorship for new professionals and programs, as well as re-emerging, existing ones. A factor to help all succeed in their missions. Just as Alcoholics Anonymous is experiencing its pioneer stages in many new countries, so will addiction treatment be a pioneering venture in these countries as well. We forget sometimes how advanced and sophisticated our treatment centers are in the U.S. compared to those in the rest of the world—where existing countries and continents have had A.A. itself for a long time. Their healthcare systems have often failed to include effective addiction treatment centers and programs. For these, the Little Hill Foundation will be honored and privileged to extend our hosting, hospitality, history, and heritage. Following A.A.'s theme, we want Alina Lodge to be there and reach out whenever anyone or any organization wants to discover, improve, or learn more about effective addiction treatment and long-term recovery.

- **Timeless Traditions**—There is a new age today: Fast everything; loss of family values; an unfortunate flight from our religious institutions; the sometimes troubling trends of secularization and self-help therapy; the drift from AA's basic reliance on our Creator and from its spiritual roots; the mental health dominated, quick fix approach to addiction treatment; and the abandonment of appropriate resources for addiction treatment by both the government and private industry. This new picture often leaves individuals and families caught in the downward spiral of addiction, finding themselves in serious trouble, and experiencing great difficulty in recovery. We believe it is therefore extremely comforting to know that there is still "A place where hope can become fact." Rooted in the founding traditions of the early AA movement, forged by a brilliant and visionary leader and business woman, Alina Lodge remains a beacon of hope for this new age and for this current century. It has a strong belief in dignity, respect, discipline, manners, family values, spiritual principles, tenets of worldwide fellowship, and a tough, compassionate approach to a deadly disease. Alina Lodge will remain committed to its heritage and traditions of excellence in clinical care for those suffering from addiction. As we move into this new millennium, we extend our hand to those in need and who still suffer so they may find their way back from the throes of addiction. We want always to be there, solid in our commitment, steadfast in our clinical integrity, and full of hope that recovery is possible. We welcome all who would like to join us in this mission, We want forever, in our hearts and actions, to express and effectuate our profound sense of gratitude to Geraldine Owen Delaney and to the 12-Step Fellowship of Alcoholics Anonymous.

Epilogue

[By the Author, Dick B.]

You've covered some unusual territory: You may have again learned significant facts about the life of the remarkable Mrs. Geraldine O. Delaney, whose initials happened to stand for "God" and for "Good Orderly Direction." They are unusual initials which prompted many, including A.A. old-timers, to speak joshingly of Mrs. D. as "God."Ironically, Mrs. D., who might well have entered A.A. as one of Bill Wilson's "agnostics," did come to believe in, and rely upon, our Creator. As to "Good Orderly Direction," she fashioned a unique, long-term, treatment that challenged her students and other rehabs to consider (or at least support) much needed new, good, orderly, *direction.* Very unusual! Very successful!

Betty Ford wrote that Mrs. D. has been a front-runner in the field of alcohol and drug treatment for many many years. Noted Rabbi Abraham J. Twerski, M.D., of Gateway Rehab in Pennsylvania, said of the First Edition of my book, that it gave a valuable account of Alina Lodge's many successes with alcoholics, addicts, and their family members through long-term education, discipline, structure and residence. Father Joseph C. Martin, S.S.--famed Roman Catholic priest who founded Ashley's in Maryland, and whose "chalk talk" films have been seen by thousands in treatment centers across America--said: (1) Of Mrs. D., "What made her and her beloved Alina Lodge so successful was her deeply passionate love of alcoholics." (2) Of our new edition, "I whole heartedly approve and endorse this tribute to her life. The title, 'Hope,' is a very accurate one indeed, for she gave hope to so many hopeless souls."

At the conclusion of this Epilogue, we've included tributes, awards, and accolades to Mrs. Delaney received during her lifetime. But, this second edition of HOPE is not about the past. When I wrote the first edition, Mrs. Delaney was alive, informative, acclaimed, and "retired." She had, at that time, been succeeded by an interim director with whom I spent much time and from whom I received much information about the Lodge philosophy and program. That director was discharged during the time I was researching at Alina. However, our first edition was able meticulously and accurately to portray Mrs. D.'s non-permissive approach to treatment. It told her story in her own words, and it reported the story of the Lodge in the words of many, including Mrs. D. It concluded with a question that could be summarized as this: Just how would the Lodge survive the loss of an executive who played such a dominant role and how could it proceed successfully after her retirement and (ultimately) her demise.

Then Mrs. D. did pass away. The present Executive Director had been hired, and I was fortunate enough to be able to meet with him in person after he had taken charge.

Under his tutelage, the Lodge has been alive with activity: It has modified its program in one major area, to include use of certain medications and to treat disorders other than chemical dependency. It has returned its student population from 30 to the 80 bed numbers of the old days. New staff have been hired to cover psychiatric, psychological, dual-disorder, marketing, and fund-raising needs. With all that, could the Delaney legacy and approach survive, be successfully applied, and be appropriately augmented with new ideas and approaches tailored to deal with the much-damaged treatment scene in America today?

To answer such questions and highlight his new leadership plans and achievements, Mark Schottinger prepared several papers for my use. They covered the Lodge's status at the time of his arrival. They detailed the Lodge program as it is now being conducted. They offered the same degree of extra hope that the Lodge had long provided to the "reluctant to recover" despite the chaos in the scene of managed care, insurance carrier, and government confusion. And–on being asked to write a new edition--I was eager to see if this new Executive Director had really grasped and furthered what I had seen when I interviewed Mrs. Delaney; talked extensively to staff, alumni, and students; and resided "on campus" for about a week.

The answers are heart-warming and positive. In this second edition, you have viewed several new achievements at Alina. You have, I trust, found still alive and well the unique Delaney approach, philosophy, and special offer of hope. You have read a factual, down-to-earth explanation of the program today. And I believe you will conclude, as I have, that Mark Schottinger has successfully grasped the helm, utilized the very best of the Lodge's program traditions, and offered assurance that Alina Lodge will continue as the place of Hope–*And* that it will retain its "send them to Alina Lodge" reputation. It will, I think you can agree, offer the indeterminate, long-term approach to the "reluctant to recover;" maintain the non-permissive toughness that reaches students in a unique and effective way; and progress vigorously with the vital funding, cost-containment, and student concerns that gave Geraldine O. Delaney and Alina Lodge their well-earned recognition.

Geraldine O. Delaney Awards and Accolades

Appointments

1949   Executive Director, Essex County Service for the Chronically Ill (renamed Chr-ill)
1957   Executive Director of Little Hill-Alina Lodge
1975   Appointed by New Jersey's Governor to its State Advisory Council on Alcohol Problems
1985   Advisory Board of the U.S. Alcohol, Drug Abuse and Mental Health Administration

Honors and Awards

1979   Woman of the Year (awarded by New Jersey Task Force on Women and Alcohol)
1980   Citizen of the Year (awarded by Carrier Foundation, New Jersey)
1982   Honorary Doctorate of Humane Letters (awarded by Seton Hall University)
1983   Knox College and Lombard College 50 Year Club Scroll of Honor
1984   SECAD Award (SECAD/10)

1987	Commendation, New Jersey Medical Society, "Treating Tobacco Dependence" Symposium
1987	Geisinger National Achievement Award (Freedom '87)
1987	Distinguished Service Award (Rutgers University Summer School of Alcohol Studies)
1987	Crawford House Award
1991	Sister Cities Award
1992	Bronze Key (Award by National Council on Alcoholism and Drug Dependence)

Posthumous Awards

1999	Southern Coastal Conference 1st Annual Geraldine O. Delaney Memorial Lecture Award
2000	NAATP 20th Century Pioneers Award

Special Tributes

"A Pioneer in the field of addiction treatment and education. Her inspiration and skill saved thousands of alcoholics, drug addicts and their families. There is no equal in the history of recovery." Conway Hunter, M.D.

"Professionals will welcome this book about the legendary Mrs. Geraldine Owen Delaney. Her message will certainly be of help to many people." Mel Schulstad, Colonel, U.S.A.F., Retired; CCD (NCAC II) Counselor; Author; Co-Founder and Past President of the National Association of Alcoholism and Drug Abuse Counselors

END

Appendix 1

PART I - ALCOHOL

Alcohol is a Central Nervous System depressant.

Alcohol is a sedative drug, an anesthetic. It puts the nervous system to sleep in a progressive order. Perhaps this comes as a surprise to those who have referred to an alcoholic drink as a "pick me up." Alcohol has meant "stimulant"' at the end of a hectic day to many people. Alcoholic beverages act like sugar and create an initial surge of energy on consumption as the level rises. However, the sedative property of alcohol takes over quickly, beginning in the one to two drink range. The first part of the brain affected is that which controls inhibitions and discretion. Chemically, that part of the brain which would register fatigue and sensitive judgment is being impaired. (One drink refers to a measure of one and one half (1 ½) ounces of 90 proof alcohol, a 12 ounce can of beer, 3 ounces of a fortified wine (e.g., sherry), or a 4 to 5 ounce glass of light table wine). Remember, alcohol is alcohol to everyone. As the drinking individual increases the intake to the three or four drink ranges, the voluntary motor system becomes affected. If the consumption raises the blood level alcohol to the vicinity of one half of one percent (.5%), the involuntary motor system can be affected to the point where life is threatened, if breathing and pulse become impaired.

Alcohol is a toxic substance.

The word "toxic" means poisonous. Alcohol is a substance foreign to the body; a substance for which the body has no use. Having been swallowed, the body functions to eliminate alcohol from the system. All of the alcohol is absorbed directly through the stomach wall and small intestinal lining into the blood stream. It will then be processed through the liver and oxidized into carbon dioxide and water for elimination. A very small percentage of unchanged alcohol will be removed through urination, respiration, and perspiration. As thorough as the liver is, however, it 'detoxifies' very slowly. The healthy liver will process only 3/4 to 1 ounce of 90 proof alcohol an hour. (Percentage of ethyl alcohol is one half (½) the proof. Example: 100 proof is 50% alcohol). Any amount in excess of this 3/4 to 1 ounce will continue to circulate through the system, including the brain until metabolized.

Alcohol is high in calories.

Ethyl alcohol has a high calorie count (one ounce of 100 proof alcohol contains about 100 calories), but no nutritional value. Most active alcoholics will consume up to 40 or 50% of their total calorie consumption in the form of alcohol. Those who drink in quantity often feel no hunger and are without the urge to eat. This often leads to poor dietary habits and can contribute to the development of health problems such as vitamin deficiencies and malnutrition.

Other depressants mixed with alcohol increase the potency.
Alcohol is but one of the forms of central nervous system depressants. There are many forms sold over the counter and by prescription in both solid and liquid forms. These include minor tranquilizers, barbiturates, pain killers, and sleeping preparations. When alcohol is combined with these a synergistic effect or potentiation can occur. This means that the combination of one drug and one drug may add up to an effect greater than the sum of the two taken drugs. This is extremely dangerous and has produced many tragic deaths for people who "didn't mean to."

Some examples of effects of drinking alcohol
The one to two drink range: For some there may be gross drinking behavior. There is markedly different behavior from a person's non-drinking variety. Some refer to it as a "Dr. Jekyll and Mr. Hyde" syndrome, More common is the change in the tone of voice or subtle attitude change. Remarks that might be delivered in a flat, non-controversial way without alcohol in the system may be spoken sarcastically, or cynically–perhaps said sharply, rudely, or punishingly. The effect in this range stems primarily from the removal of inhibitions. It has been said, "alcohol doesn't make people do things, but it allows them to do a heck of a lot". Self-consciousness melts. The "courage" to speak one's mind pops up miraculously. Conviction that "I'm right and they are wrong" may come to the fore. Important to remember is that these phenomena are the result of the sedation of the part of the brain which controls behavior in *anyone* who drinks alcohol.

Three to four drink range: (Example: two cocktails and a glass of wine with the meal.) At this stage the voluntary motor system is becoming affected. As in the one to two drink range the effects for most will be subtle and gradual. For some, however, there will be noticeable loss of coordination or perhaps speech impairment. Most of the common results in this stage nest cozily under the blanket of "accidents". The "accidents" referred to are more in the nature of social indiscretions, though "head on collisions" count, too. Accidently knocked over water glasses at a dinner party, leaning glasses half on and half off a coaster, brushing against people while moving from one place to another, burning holes in pants, skirts, yours or theirs, unaware. Naturally, these things sometimes occur in the lives of non-drinkers, too, but if a person has been drinking in this range the culprit is most likely alcohol producing a loss of eye/hand coordination. It is important to keep in mind that as this sedation process is progressing, the drinker is becoming the one least aware of the drug's true effect, Hence, drinkers, alcoholic or non-alcoholic, can become argumentative, stubborn, and obstinate at this juncture, and never believe that they are "that bad".

Further drinking: Beyond the aforementioned range, drinking effects become increasingly noticeable. A staggering gait or slurred speech may be the symptom. Loss of consciousness ("passing out") may result. In the extreme, life threatening consequences may occur. Remember, these are effects of alcohol to which alcoholic and non-alcoholic alike are equally susceptible.

PART 11 - ALCOHOLISM

"Alcoholism is a complex disease". This statement was made by the American Medical Association in 1956.

"Alcoholism is a *chronic, progressive, and potentially fatal disease.* It is characterized by tolerance and physical dependency, pathologic organ changes, or both, all of which are the direct consequences of alcohol ingested."* This statement was developed jointly by the National Council on Alcoholism and the American Medical Society on Alcoholism Committee on Definitions and published in the Annals of Internal Medicine, December Issue, 1976.

Alcoholism is chronic

Alcoholism being "chronic" means that the physical, emotional, and social changes that occur persist over a long period of time and may be cumulative. It is indicative that the disease does not go away no matter how long it has been arrested. Any ingestion of alcohol or the alcohol family of drugs may reactivate alcoholism–the disease. This may be more clearly understood looking at another chronic disease, diabetes. If the diabetic does not continue the prescribed regimen, he knows that an active, acute episode may occur. Hence, we do not talk about someone as "having been diabetic"; so, too, with alcoholics. People are alcoholics once the disease has been established, whether the disease is active or arrested.

Alcoholism is progressive

Alcoholism is progressive in two ways. First, it is progressive in that the longer the alcoholism is active, the worse things become. This is best described in the study done by Dr. E.M. Jellinek of the World Health Organization. This progression begins with things like drinking behavior which is markedly different from a person's non-drinking behavior, preoccupation with drinking, gulping and sneaking drinks, blackouts (a true temporary amnesia during which the drinker may have functioned nearly normally but afterward has no recall or memory of thought and actions which occurred), and large drinking capacity for many in the pre-alcoholic stages. It continues as alcoholism progresses with a loss of control. Alibis about drinking and behavior begin. Eye-openers (not necessarily a morning drink, but any consumption of alcohol used, to provide initiative or motivation or to stabilize motor control such as reducing tremors or "shakes"), changing the pattern, antisocial behavior, loss of friends and/or job, and possibly seeking medical help enter the picture. In the later stages, binges or ⁻benders (prolonged drinking episodes frequently following attempts at abstinence or control such as going on the wagon or giving it up for Lent, etc.) may be experienced. Shakes and/or tremors, protecting the supply, unreasonable resentments, nameless fears and anxieties, and the collapse of the alibi system occur. This progression terminates one of three ways: 1) death, 2) permanent institutionalization or 3) recovery if diagnosed and treated.

The second aspect of progression, very important to alcoholics and family alike, is the understanding that the disease progresses even in sobriety. If an alcoholic resumes the use of any mood or mind changing chemicals after a period of abstinence it will not be like starting over again or picking up where he or she left off. Rather it will be like picking up where he would have been had he been drinking through the period of sobriety. This is documented in many case studies. It is like a leaky fuel supply. If you put a spark to the few accumulated drips you have a fire. If you put out the fire and remove the threat of the spark, but do nothing about the leak, and return with the same size spark two years later, you will have a holocaust.

Alcoholism is irreversible

Alcoholics cannot return to social drinking. Although therapy, education, and continuing involvement with Alcoholics Anonymous help arrest alcoholism and assist in the maintenance of sobriety, they are not a *cure*. There is no cure for this disease. It is merely in remission.

Alcoholism is a complex disease.

"Complex" means that every area of a person's being comes into play in the process. Physically there is addiction with dependency and tolerance. Mentally there is deterioration of clear, sound thought. Spiritually there is increasing bankruptcy. This ability to feel part of something greater than self is usually something that leaves early in the disease and returns late in recovery. As one doctor puts it, in alcoholism "there is a personality or emotional imbalance which is chemically induced". The active alcoholic tries to control and keep a life of normalcy, but cannot do so because of his or her addiction. As episodes become more severe, longer in duration, and closer together any semblance of normalcy vanishes. The alcoholic with alcohol in the system cannot by a simple "making up his mind" or using "will power" control the drinking and its results. Alcohol is in control. Hence, the alibis or excuses increase and denial deepens. The result is a continued march down the scale of progression. Critical in the understanding of this is the fact that this is a chemically induced phenomena. Life becomes unmanageable because a chemical is in control, not the alcoholic or the family. It should be noted that when abstinence becomes established, control in the form of the narrowing of mood swings and disciplined thinking *returns slowly*.

The cause of alcoholism is unknown.

No one knows at this time what causes alcoholism. We know that it exists, that it is diagnosable and treatable. Researchers have been delving into many facets of the disease trying to determine cause. To date the results are inconclusive. Among the leading theories are those pertaining to the presence or absence of enzymes which might impede the proper functioning of the oxidation process by the liver, a differential blood factor which may be tested for even some time after the alcohol is out of the blood stream, and genetics. It is the strong feeling of many that "the cause" will be a combination of factors rather than one thing alone.

Alcoholism is not self-inflicted.

People do not wake up and decide to become alcoholic. This is a disease that can afflict anyone who has the physical make up. It is not a respecter of social class, nationality, educational background, economic status, or upbringing. The only true or guaranteed preventative is abstinence. We have no tests to determine ahead of time who will become alcoholic. Gross complications may be prevented through early diagnosis and with the willingness and acceptance of that alcoholic person to accept and use treatment.

Appendix 2

What Can I Do to Help?

The statement that family members can be of no assistance to the alcoholic's recovery is misleading. The desire to aid in the alcoholic's recovery is a natural and healthy one. Upon hearing that there is nothing family members can do to affect recovery, there are often feelings of disappointment, frustration, and of being left out.

Responsibility for the alcoholic's recovery rests with the alcoholic. Success or failure in recovery depends upon the continuing quality of his or her decision to remain totally abstinent. All others are powerless over the alcoholic's decision to choose abstinence or continued addiction. This decision is made within an environment, however. There are things family members can do to contribute either positively or negatively to this "Environment of Recovery."

Here are some suggestions for specific things family members can do that will make important contributions to a healthy, constructive Environment of Recovery.

1.   **BECOME   EDUCATED   ABOUT   THE   DISEASE   OF ALCOHOLISM/POLY-ADDICTION AND RECOVERY.**

Each person approaches recovery with opinions and attitudes about alcohol, drinking, mood and mind changing medication and about the changes needed. These opinions and attitudes are the result of trying one's best to understand what is going on in his or her life. Unfortunately, we do not always have the facts in our grasp when developing our understanding. Without the facts we have no idea what we are dealing with, and our efforts to help in recovery can only end in confusion and frustration for both ourselves and the alcoholic. Facts about the Disease of Alcoholism, or Sedativism as it is often called, and the recovery process are readily available from:

a.   **Literature Provided by Little Hill-Alina Lodge** - Read all material thoughtfully and with an open mind. Since some of this information is new to you, and perhaps in conflict with your present opinions and attitudes, careful rereadings are strongly recommended.

b.   **The Family Program** - A series of lectures, discussions, films, and counseling sessions is designed for your education. Consistent attendance will be extremely beneficial

159

to participants who approach the program with an open, searching mind. Education for the family is the basis for permitting visiting.

     c.   **Al-Anon Meetings** - These meetings in your community provide persons living close to an active or recovering alcoholic an opportunity to share their experience in living with alcoholism and addiction. A great wealth of practical information is available through the discussion format. Free literature is provided at these meetings.

     d.   **Alateen Meetings** - These meetings in your community provide an opportunity for teenaged friends and relatives of alcoholics to learn about alcoholism and its effects on their lives. Free literature is provided at these meetings.

     e.   **Families Anonymous Meetings** - This is a 12 Step support group primarily for the parents of addicted children. Though not as widely available as Al-Anon, there may be a chapter in your area. Like Al-Anon, Families Anonymous publishes much free literature.

     f.   **Adult Children of Alcoholics Meetings** - This 12 Step Fellowship is for adults who grew up in a home with alcoholism in one or both parents. If you already have a background in Al-Anon, and are the adult child of an alcoholic, you may find these meetings especially helpful.

     g.   **Open Meetings of Alcoholics Anonymous** - Many meetings of Alcoholics Anonymous are open to the general public. You can gain much firsthand knowledge and many new insights from hearing what recovering alcoholics have to say about themselves and their experiences with the Disease of Alcoholism.

     h.   **The Book,** *Alcoholics Anonymous* - This is the basic text of A.A. The book contains information on the Disease of Alcoholism and recovery from it. It is available from public libraries and may be purchased at most open A.A. meetings.

     i.   **The In-Residence Family Program at Little Hill-Alina Lodge** - This part of our treatment program is designed to provide in-depth education about alcoholism and addiction and your role as a family member. Should you be invited to participate in this phase of our program, be sure to give it the highest priority.

2.   START TO LISTEN

Replacing fiction with new facts is impossible until we begin to listen. Steadily expanding knowledge is important to a wholesome "Environment of Recovery." With the arrival of sobriety, attitudes, actions and reactions of the alcoholic and of all family members are likely to be vulnerable to emotional extremes. Unless you make a conscious effort to listen to what is actually being said, you are likely to increase the static in the lines of communication. Good listening helps put objective thought between impulses and actions.

You are **NOT** listening IF:

 a.   **Your mind is busy arranging arguments against new ideas.** Automatic rejection of new concepts simply because they conflict with your present beliefs is a surefire way of avoiding learning and growth.

 b.   **You are more concerned with what you are going to say than with what is being said.** Assuming your own statements are more important than what another may have to say makes a one-way street out of communication. Such assumptions only destroy opportunities to communicate.

 c.   **You assume you already know what another is going to say.** Basing expectations for the present on another's past performance makes no allowance for the change and growth that are an essential part of everyone's recovery.

 d.   **You so belittle another that you have no respect for whatever he or she may be saying.** The assumption that the alcoholic is always wrong and sober family members are always right is a common one. This attitude was inappropriate when the alcoholic was drinking, and is even more so now, with recovery under way. No one is always right or always wrong.

To get the real benefit from Al-Anon/Alateen/Open Meetings or any of the 12 Step Fellowships, it is important to listen for the many similarities you will find in the feelings and attitudes expressed. Identify with other group members. One can easily find superficial differences between oneself and others. Looking for such differences only isolates you from the group and severely restricts the power of these groups to lead you toward recovery.

Stopping to listen intently, thoughtfully, and with a fully open mind to what is really being said may well be a new experience for you. It will take constant awareness and self-discipline to break old thinking habits and develop new ones, but the results will be well worth the effort.

3.   START LIVING A STRUCTURED DAY

It is common in households disturbed by alcoholism and addiction for much of the structure and order to collapse. The family lives increasingly from crisis to crisis, with most actions and reactions dictated by the momentary condition of the alcoholic. Expenditure of so much emergency energy creates emotional exhaustion in the family. Often there is a heavy sense of frustration and guilt as routine but important matters go unattended.

Working to introduce some structure into your day will ease the sense of disorganization and frenzy. It will contribute to your peace of mind and emotional health. Developing your own sense of structure and order -- not a rigid schedule, but rather a consistent shape to your daily activities-- may prove contagious. Other family members may lean toward the more comfortable regularity you are building into your own living. For the recovering alcoholic such structure is essential.

Developing this sort of structure would include:

      a.   **Eating Regular Meals** -Try to schedule reasonably consistent meal times. Make it a point to eat three nutritionally balanced meals each day. Make taking vitamins part of your daily routine, particularly B complex and C unless medically contradicted. Eliminate caffeine and nicotine intake.

      b.   **Establishing Regular Bed and Rising Times** - Ample sleep on a consistent basis is essential to your emotional and physical well-being. The only practical way of achieving this is by sticking to a sensible rest schedule.

      c.   **Planning Brief Rest Periods** - Rarely is a schedule so crammed that there is no room for a rest break of perhaps 15 or 20 minutes, a period during which you can shut off the world, By interrupting the flow of the day's activities you may give yourself the opportunity to get back in touch with yourself. Relaxation periods, meditation, or prayer, all help to regain your physical, emotional, and spiritual strength. If this is only a few minutes in duration, these two minute vacations will do much to help you maintain a healthy, constructive outlook during the balance of the day.

      d.   **Framing Out the Plan of Your Day** - Before you start each day, make an outline of several specific things you would like to accomplish during the morning and afternoon. It is important that these goals be practical and realistic for the allotted time. If one goal is a major project, break it down into segments, treating each as a separate task.

It is important to accept that some, or perhaps all, of the scheduled activities may not be completed as originally planned. In this case, they are simply rescheduled for another time. This is an activities guideline, not a timetable. Be flexible!

Try to arrange your schedule into short-term compartments. In this way, if the morning's schedule is not fulfilled, the afternoon's schedule need not be affected.

By giving each of your days an overall regulated but flexible shape, you will bring a new level of order into your life, which will have a positive impact on those around you.

Moreover, the alcoholic is learning to live a more structured day as part of the program of recovery. By bringing this new structure into your own life, you will be reinforcing this effort in addition to helping yourself.

4. BEGIN PRACTICING CONSISTENCY

Everyone, especially you, will benefit from your efforts to be more consistent in your attitudes and more dependable in your actions and reactions.

Inconsistencies, such as shifting your position to accommodate the mood of the moment or backing down on threats or promises, contribute to a sense of uncertainty and instability. This is definitely detrimental to the "Environment of Recovery."

Check your standards and motives in terms of your own needs and conscience. Be sure they are your own standards, rather than those you feel you ought to have, or ones that have been imposed upon you by others. Once satisfied, stand by them, not with self-righteous inflexibility, but with the intelligent awareness of the importance of clearly established, reasonable limits to behavior.

Avoid making threats or promises you will be either unwilling or unable to carry out. Think carefully before making any commitments you might later regret. Remember there are consequences both good and bad to all decisions.

It is helpful for all concerned to live within a "ring of reality. " By this we mean that each of us needs to feel the consequences of our attitudes, decisions, and actions to know whether they are right for us or not. Inconsistencies in your actions or reactions constitute gaps in the ring. You become an enabler of others to live removed from reality without appropriate consequences. Dependable responses and sticking to standards will discourage manipulation by others and contribute to a constructive, stable, and secure atmosphere.

5. INVESTIGATE YOURSELF

Family members have generally become so preoccupied with alcohol and the alcoholic, they have lost touch with their attitudes and feelings about themselves. They are unaware of the changes taking place within themselves over the years of exposure to active alcoholism and attendant problems.

Do you know your true feelings? Are you managing them or are they managing you? What are your attitudes toward the alcoholic, toward life in general, and toward yourself? What are your attitudes toward the Disease of Alcoholism? Your emotional stability and growth depend largely upon the answers to these questions. You can be of help to no one until you have come to grips with yourself. Here are some suggestions:

a.   **Write Your Life Story** - A good place to start this self-investigation is by writing YOUR "Life Story." This is a simple, written account of the events of your life from as far back as you can remember up to the present. It deals with what happened and how you felt, with no attempt to analyze why you may have felt the way you did or acted the way you did. Be honest and direct as you can, remembering only you will ever read it. (Be sure it isn't left around for curious eyes.) Some find that writing in the third person, using "he" or "she" rather than "I" makes objectivity easier.

Write a little each day, and leave a note indicating where you left off. Do not reread the story as it progresses. When you are finished, put the piece away for a week or so to let it get cold. Then read it straight through, if possible without interruption, underlining those areas to which you might want to give further, more detailed thought. The result of this reading will most certainly provide some highly significant new insights into yourself and into your real feelings, attitudes, and self-image throughout your life and now.

Ask Yourself Three Questions:

(1)   What am I now bringing to the family unit?

What are the contributions - material, emotional, and spiritual - you are making now? (Define all terms you use, i.e., what do you mean by spiritual?) A few areas to consider might be: financial support, housework, meal planning and preparation, thrift, responsibility, leadership, consideration of others, sound judgment, patience, emotional stability, courage and love. Others might be: anxiety, anger, resentment, extravagance, thoughtlessness, nagging or confusion. Make the list of both positive and negative items as complete and as honest as you can. Then review it, and ask yourself:

(2)   What would I like to bring to the family unit?

What items are on the list that you wish were not there, and what items are missing that you would like to have there? There are two hazards: (1) make sure the things you would like to add to the list are not so idealized as to be humanly impossible and (2) make sure your wishes are based upon your own standards, rather than on what you think you ought to bring or would look good to others. Then ask yourself:

(3)   What can I do now to improve my contribution to the family unit?

What attitudes and qualities do you have to develop or improve? From the answers to Question two develop your own "Plan of Action." Your Plan will include a list of specific attitudes and behavior patterns you need to work on, as well as the means you will use to work on them.

With this new awareness of areas in your life that you have decided to improve, you can concentrate on your own self development program, rather than wasting your energies and time in the futile effort of trying to govern the alcoholic or supervise recovery for him or her.

6. TAKE A DAILY LOOK AT YOURSELF

As you follow this course of self-improvement, schedule a checkpoint into the structure of your day. As each day closes, look back and ask yourself, "How did I do today?" Compare your thoughts, attitudes, and actions of the day with what you would like them to be. By taking this daily pause for reflection and review, you will see your progress toward the goals you have set for yourself, and you will be able to identify the frequently recurring problems that may require more concentrated effort. You can also detect any drifts in attitudes and thinking before they approach unmanageable proportions.

7. INCLUDE THE CONCEPT OF A HIGHER POWER IN YOUR LIFE

The loss of a sense of being a part of something greater than oneself, or spiritual bankruptcy, is as common in nonalcoholic family members as it is in alcoholics. In both cases it is the source of many profound difficulties.

A major symptom of this bankruptcy is the conviction that everything, particularly the alcoholic's continuing abstinence, is your responsibility. You can be of little help to the alcoholic as long as you believe that recovery depends on your doing all the right things.

In the beginning of recovery this may be a difficult area to deal with. Don't force it! Try, a day at a time, to place increasing trust and reliance on something outside yourself. A good friend, a group of people, a counselor will do to start. Then, gradually, you may find benefit in trying prayer, reading spiritually oriented literature or returning to a past faith. Remember, Easy Does It'.

These recommendations may not coincide with your own ideas of how to help the alcoholic. Many years of practical experience have shown it is only in ways such as these - it is only in working to create a healthy, stable, secure "Environment of Recovery" - that a family member can truly contribute to the recovering alcoholic's progress.

You have the choice of either hanging on to your previous options and practices to deal with alcoholism and recovery, or of turning to this new path of building an atmosphere that is more conducive to serenity and peaceful living by working on yourself. With the former you become or remain part of the problem; with the latter you become part of the solution. It's up to you!

Bibliography

Al-Anon Faces Alcoholism. 2d ed. New York: Al-Anon Family Group Headquarters, 1989.

Alcoholics Anonymous. 1st ed. New York City: Works Publishing Company, 1939.

———. 3d ed. New York City: Alcoholics Anonymous World Services, Inc., 1976.

_____. 4th ed. New York City. Alcoholics Anonymous World Services, Inc., 2001.

Authorized (King James) Version. New York: Thomas Nelson, 1984.

B., Dick. *Anne Smith's Journal, 1933-1939: A.A.'s Principles of Success, 3rd ed.,* Kihei, Hi: Paradise Research Publications, Inc., 1998.

_____. *By the Power of God: A Guide to Early A.A. Groups & Forming Similar Groups Today.* Kihei, HI: Paradise Research Publications, Inc., 2000.

———. *Dr. Bob and His Library: Books For Twelve Step Growth:* Kihei: HI: Paradise Research Publications, Inc., 1998.

_____. *God and Alcoholism.* Kihei, HI: Paradise Research Publications, Inc., 2002.

_____. *Good Morning!: Quiet Time, Morning Watch, Meditation, and Early A.A..,* 2d ed., Kihei, HI: Paradise Research Publications, Inc., 1998.

_____. *Making Known the Biblical History and Roots of Alcoholics Anonymous: An Eleven-Year Research, Writing, Publishing, and Fact Dissemination Project.* Kihei, HI: Paradise Research Publications, Inc., 2001.

———. *New Light on Alcoholism: God, Sam Shoemaker, and A.A..,* 2d ed., Kihei, HI: Paradise Research Publications, Inc., 1999.

———. *That Amazing Grace: The Role of Clarence and Grace S. in Alcoholics Anonymous.* San Rafael, CA: Paradise Research Publications, 1996.

———. *The Akron Genesis of Alcoholics Anonymous.* Newton ed. Kihei, HI: Paradise Research Publications, Inc., 1998.

———. *The Books Early AAs Read for Spiritual Growth.* 7th ed. Kihei, HI: Paradise Research Publications, Inc., 1998.

_____. *The Golden Text of A.A.: God, the Pioneers, and Real Spirituality.* Kihei, HI: Paradise Research Publications, Inc., 1999.

———. *The Good Book and The Big Book: A.A.'s Roots in the Bible.* Bridge Builders ed. Kihei, HI: Paradise Research Publications, Inc., 1997.

———. *The Oxford Group and Alcoholics Anonymous: A Design for Living That Works,* 2d ed., Kihei, HI: Paradise Research Publications, Inc., 1998.

———. *Turning Point: A History of Early A.A.'s Spiritual Roots and Successes.* San Rafael, CA: Paradise Research Publications, 1997.

_____. *Utilizing Early A.A.'s Spiritual Roots for Recovery Today.* Kihei, HI: Paradise Research Publications, Inc., 1998.

167

_____. *Why Early A.A. Succeeded: The Good Book in Alcoholics Anonymous Yesterday and Today (A Bible Study Primer for AAs and Other 12-Steppers)*. Kihei, HI: Paradise Research Publications, Inc., 2001.

———, and Bill Pittman. *Courage to Change: The Christian Roots of the 12-Step Movement*. Grand Rapids, MI: Fleming H. Revell, 1994.

B., Mel. *New Wine: The Spiritual Roots of the Twelve Step Miracle*. Center City, MN: Hazelden Foundation, 1991.

Clinebell, Howard. *Understanding and Counseling Persons with Alcohol, Drug, and Behavioral Addictions*. Rev. and enl. ed., Nashville: Abingdon Press, 1998.

Daily Reflections. New York: Alcoholics Anonymous World Services, Inc., 1990.

DR. BOB and the Good Oldtimers. New York: Alcoholics Anonymous World Services, Inc., 1980.

Hart, Stan. *Rehab: A Comprehensive Guide to Recommended Drug-Alcohol Treatment Centers in the United States*. New York: Harper & Row, 1988.

Jellinek, E. M. *The Disease Concept of Alcoholism*. New Haven, CT: College and University Press, 1960.

Kurtz, Ernest. *Not-God: A History of Alcoholics Anonymous*. Exp. ed. Center City, MN: Hazelden Educational Materials, 1991.

Landry, Mim J. *Overview of Addiction Treatment Effectiveness*. Rev. ed. 1997. U.S. Department of Health and Human Services.

Language of the Heart, The: Bill W. 's Grapevine Writings. New York: The AA Grapevine, Inc., 1988.

Lois Remembers: Memoirs of the co-founder of Al-Anon and wife of the co-founder of Alcoholics Anonymous. New York: Al-Anon Family Group Headquarters, 1987.

Ragge, Ken. *More Revealed: A Critical Analysis of Alcoholics Anonymous and the Twelve Steps*. Henderson, NV: Alert Publishing, 1991.

S., Clarence. *My Higher Power–The Lightbulb*. 2d ed. Altamonte Springs, FL: Stephen Foreman, 1985.

Self-Help Sourcebook, The. Compiled and edited by Barbara White and Edward Madara. Denville, NJ: American Self-Help Clearinghouse, 1995.

Tiebout, Harry. 1952. Surrender Versus Compliance in Therapy with Special Reference to Alcoholism. New York: The National Council on Alcoholism, n.d. First published in *Quarterly Journal of Studies on Alcohol*. Vol. 14, No. 1, March, 1953, pp. 58-68.

Twelve Steps and Twelve Traditions. New York: Alcoholics Anonymous World Services, Inc., 1952.

Twenty-Four Hours a Day. Rev. ed. Center City, MN: Hazelden Foundation, 1975.

Vaillant, George. *The Natural History of Alcoholism Revisited*. Cambridge, MA: Harvard University Press, 1995.

White, William L. *Slaying The Dragon: The History of Addiction Treatment and Recovery in America*. Bloomington, IL: Chestnut Health Systems, 1998

Way Home, The: A Spiritual Approach to Recovery. Orlando, FL: Bridge Builders, Inc., 1996.

Wilson, Jan R., and Judith A. Wilson. *Addictionary: A Primer of Recovery Terms and Concepts from Abstinence to Withdrawal*. New York: Simon and Schuster, 1992.

Index

169

Dick B.'s Historical Titles on Early A.A.'s Spiritual Roots and Successes

Anne Smith's Journal, 1933-1939 (3rd Edition)
Fwd. by Robert R. Smith, son of Dr. Bob & Anne; co-author, *Children of the Healer.*
Dr. Bob's wife, Anne, kept a journal in the 1930's from which she shared with early AAs and their families ideas from the Bible and the Oxford Group. Her ideas substantially influenced A.A.'s program. Paradise Research Publications, Inc.; 180 pp.; 6 x 9; perfect bound; 1998; $16.95; ISBN 1-885803-24-9.
By the Power of God: A Guide to Early A.A. Groups & Forming Similar Groups Today
Fwd. by Ozzie Lepper, Pres./Managing Dir., The Wilson House, East Dorset, VT.
Precise details of early A.A.'s spiritual practices—from the recollections of Grace S., widow of A.A. pioneer, Clarence S. Paradise Research Pub; 260 pp.; 6 x 9; perfect bound; 2000; $16.95; ISBN 1-885803-30-3.
Dr. Bob and His Library: A Major A.A. Spiritual Source (3rd Edition)
Fwd. by Ernest Kurtz, Ph.D., Author, *Not-God: A History of Alcoholics Anonymous.*
A study of the immense spiritual reading of the Bible, Christian literature, and Oxford Group books done and recommended by A.A. co-founder, Dr. Robert H. Smith. Paradise Research Pub., Inc.; 156 pp.; 6 x 9; perfect bound; $15.95; 1998; ISBN 1-885803-25-7.
Good Morning!: Quiet Time, Morning Watch, Meditation, and Early A.A. (2d Ed.)
A practical guide to Quiet Time—considered a "must" in early A.A. Also discusses biblical roots, history, helpful books, and how to. Paradise Research Pub; 154 pp.; 6 x 9; perfect bound; 1998; $16.95; ISBN: 1-885803-22-2.
New Light on Alcoholism: God, Sam Shoemaker, and A.A. (Second Edition)
Forewords by Nickie Shoemaker Haggart, daughter of Sam Shoemaker; Julia Harris; and Karen Plavan, Ph.D.
A comprehensive history and analysis of the all-but-forgotten specific contributions to A.A. spiritual principles and practices by New York's famous Episcopal preacher, the Rev. Dr. Samuel M. Shoemaker, Jr.—dubbed by Bill W. a "co-founder" of A.A. and credited by Bill as the well-spring of A.A.'s spiritual recovery ideas. Paradise Research Pub., Inc.; approx. 672 pp.; 6 x 9; perfect bound; 1999; $24.95; ISBN 1-885803-27-3.
The Akron Genesis of Alcoholics Anonymous (Newton Edition)
Foreword by former U.S. Congressman John F. Seiberling of Akron, Ohio.
The story of A.A.'s birth at Dr. Bob's Home in Akron on June 10, 1935. Tells what early AAs did in their meetings, homes, and hospital visits; what they read; how their ideas developed from the Bible, Oxford Group, and Christian literature. Depicts roles of A.A. founders and their wives; Henrietta Seiberling; and T. Henry Williams. Paradise Research Publications, Inc.; 400 pp., 6 x 9; perfect bound; 1998; $17.95; ISBN 1-885803-17-6.
The Books Early AAs Read for Spiritual Growth (7th Edition)
Foreword by former U.S. Congressman John F. Seiberling of Akron, Ohio.
The most exhaustive bibliography (with brief summaries) of all the books known to have been read and recommended for spiritual growth by early AAs in Akron and on the East Coast. Paradise Research Publications, Inc.; 126 pp.; 6 x 9; perfect bound; 1998; $15.95; ISBN 1-885803-26-5.
The Golden Text of A.A.: God, the Pioneers, and Real Spirituality
This booklet is the second of a series containing the remarks of Dick B. at his annual seminars at The Wilson House. The booklet contains the sincere and surprising credit that Bill Wilson and Bill Dotson (A.A. #3) gave to God for curing them of the disease of alcoholism.; 94pp; 6 x 9; perfect bound; 2000; $14.95; ISBN 1-885803-29-X.
The Good Book and The Big Book: A.A.'s Roots in the Bible (Second Edition)
Fwd. by Robert R. Smith, son of Dr. Bob & Anne; co-author, *Children of the Healer.*

The author shows conclusively that A.A.'s program of recovery came primarily from the Bible. This is a history of A.A.'s biblical roots as they can be seen in A.A.'s Big Book, Twelve Steps, and Fellowship. Paradise Research Publications, Inc.; 264 pp.; 6 x 9; perfect bound; 1997; $17.95; ISBN 1-885803-16-8.

The Oxford Group & Alcoholics Anonymous   (Second Edition)
          Foreword by Rev. T. Willard Hunter; author, columnist, Oxford Group activist.
A comprehensive history of the origins, principles, practices, and contributions to A.A. of "A First Century Christian Fellowship" (also known as the Oxford Group) of which A.A. was an integral part in the developmental period between 1931 and 1939. Paradise Research Publications, Inc.; 432 pp.; 6 x 9; perfect bound; 1998; $17.95; ISBN 1-885803-19-2. (Previous title: *Design for Living*).

That Amazing Grace: The Role of Clarence and Grace S. in Alcoholics Anonymous
          Foreword by Harold E. Hughes, former U.S. Senator from, and Governor of, Iowa.
Precise details of early A.A.'s spiritual practices—from the recollections of Grace S., widow of A.A. pioneer, Clarence S. Paradise Research Pub; 160 pp.; 6 x 9; perfect bound; 1996; $16.95; ISBN 1-885803-06-0.

Turning Point: A History of Early A.A.'s Spiritual Roots and Successes
          Fwd. by Paul Wood, Ph.D., Pres., Nat. Council on Alcoholism and Drug Dependence. *Turning Point* is a comprehensive history of early A.A.'s spiritual roots and successes. It is the culmination of six years of research, traveling, and interviews. Dick B.'s latest title shows specifically what the Twelve Step pioneers borrowed from: (1) The Bible; (2) The Rev. Sam Shoemaker's teachings; (3) The Oxford Group; (4) Anne Smith's Journal; and (5) meditation periodicals and books, such as *The Upper Room*. Paradise Research Publications, Inc.; 776 pp.; 6 x 9; perfect bound; 1997; $29.95; ISBN: 1-885803-07-9.

Utilizing Early A.A.'s Spiritual Roots for Recovery Today
This booklet is the first of a series containing the remarks of Dick B. at his annual seminars at The Wilson House—birthplace of A.A. co-founder Bill Wilson. It is intended as a guide for study groups who wish to apply today the highly successful program and principles of early A.A.. Paradise Research Publications, Inc.; 106 pp.; 6 x 9; perfect bound; 2000; $14.95; ISBN 1-885803-28-1.

Why Early A.A. Succeeded: The Good Book in Alcoholics Anonymous Yesterday and Today
          Foreword by Jeffrey H. Boyd, M.D., M. Div., M.P.H.; Chairman of Psychiatry, Waterbury Hospital, Waterbury, CT; Ordained Episcopal Minister; Chairman of the New England Evangelical Theological Society.
Paradise Research Pub; approx 330 pp.; 6 x 9; perfect bound; 2001; $17.95; ISBN 1-885803-31-1.

About the Author

Dick B. writes books on the spiritual roots of Alcoholics Anonymous. They show how the basic and highly successful biblical ideas used by early AAs can be valuable tools for success in today's A.A. His research can also help the religious and recovery communities work more effectively with alcoholics, addicts, and others involved in Twelve Step programs.

The author is an active, recovered member of A.A.; a retired attorney; and a Bible student. He has sponsored more than eighty men in their recovery from alcoholism. Consistent with A.A.'s traditions of anonymity, he uses the pseudonym "Dick B."

He has had fifteen titles published: *Dr. Bob and His Library*; *Anne Smith's Journal, 1933-1939*; *The Oxford Group & Alcoholics Anonymous: A Design for Living That Works*; *The Akron Genesis of Alcoholics Anonymous*; *The Books Early AAs Read for Spiritual Growth*; *New Light on Alcoholism: God, Sam Shoemaker, and A.A.*; *Courage to Change* (with Bill Pittman); *The Good Book and The Big Book: A.A.'s Roots in the Bible*; *That Amazing Grace: The Role of Clarence and Grace S. in Alcoholics Anonymous*; *Good Morning!: Quiet Time, Morning Watch, Meditation, and Early A.A.*; *Turning Point: A History of Early A.A.'s Spiritual Roots and Successes, Hope!: The Story of Geraldine D., Alina Lodge & Recovery, Utilizing Early A.A.'s Spiritual Roots for Recovery Today, The Golden Text of A.A.*, and *By the Power of God: A Guide to Early A.A. Groups & Forming Similar Groups Today*. The books have been the subject of newspaper articles, and have been reviewed in *Library Journal, Bookstore Journal, For a Change, The Living Church, Faith at Work, Sober Times, Episcopal Life, Recovery News, Ohioana Quarterly, The PHOENIX, MRA Newsletter*, and the *Saint Louis University Theology Digest*.

Dick is the father of two married sons (Ken and Don) and a grandfather. As a young man, he did a stint as a newspaper reporter. He attended the University of California, Berkeley, where he received his A.A. degree, majored in economics, and was elected to Phi Beta Kappa in his Junior year. In the United States Army, he was an Information-Education Specialist. He received his A.B. and J.D. degrees from Stanford University, and was Case Editor of the Stanford Law Review. Dick became interested in Bible study in his childhood Sunday School and was much inspired by his mother's almost daily study of Scripture. He joined, and was president of, a Community Church affiliated with the United Church of Christ. By 1972, he was studying the origins of the Bible and began traveling abroad in pursuit of that subject. In 1979, he became much involved in a Biblical research, teaching, and fellowship ministry. In his community life, he was president of a merchants' council, Chamber of Commerce, church retirement center, and homeowners' association. He served on a public district board and was active in a service club.

In 1986, he was felled by alcoholism, gave up his law practice, and began recovery as a member of Alcoholics Anonymous. In 1990, his interest in A.A.'s Christian roots was sparked by his attendance at A.A.'s International Convention in Seattle. He has traveled widely; researched at archives, and at public and seminary libraries; interviewed scholars, historians, clergy, A.A. "old-timers" and survivors; and participated in programs on A.A.'s roots.

The author owns Good Book Publishing Co. and has several works in progress. Much of his research and writing is done in collaboration with his older son, Ken, who holds B.A., B.Th., and M.A. degrees. Ken has been a lecturer in New Testament Greek at a Bible college and a lecturer in Fundamentals of Oral Communication at San Francisco State University.

Dick belongs to the American Historical Association, Maui Writers Guild, Christian Association for Psychological Studies, Alcohol and Temperance History Group, The Authors' Guild. He is available for conferences, panels, seminars, and interviews.

How to Order Dick B.'s Historical Titles on Early A.A.

Order Form

Qty.

Send: ____ *Anne Smith's Journal, 1933-1939*	@ $16.95 ea.	$_____
____ *By the Power of God* (early A.A. groups today)	@ $16.95 ea.	$_____
____ *Dr. Bob and His Library*	@ $15.95 ea.	$_____
____ *Good Morning!* (Quiet Time, etc.)	@ $16.95 ea.	$_____
____ *New Light on Alcoholism* (Sam Shoemaker)	@ $24.95 ea.	$_____
____ *The Akron Genesis of Alcoholics Anonymous*	@ $17.95 ea.	$_____
____ *The Books Early AAs Read for Spiritual Growth*	@ $15.95 ea.	$_____
____ *The Golden Text of A.A.*	@ $14.95 ea.	$_____
____ *The Good Book and The Big Book* (Bible roots)	@ $17.95 ea.	$_____
____ *The Oxford Group & Alcoholics Anonymous*	@ $17.95 ea.	$_____
____ *That Amazing Grace* (Clarence and Grace S.)	@ $16.95 ea.	$_____
____ *Turning Point* (a comprehensive history)	@ $29.95 ea.	$_____
____ *Utilizing Early A.A.'s Spiritual Roots ... Today*	@ $14.95 ea.	$_____
____ *Why Early A.A. Succeeded*	@ $17.95 ea.	$_____

[For 14 vol. Set, put $199.95 in "Subtotal" & $25.00 in S&H]   Subtotal $_____

Shipping and Handling (within the U.S.)**   Shipping and Handling (S&H) $_____
Add 10% of retail price (minimum $4.50)
** Please contact us for S&H charges for non-U.S. orders   Total Enclosed $_____

Name: _____ (as it appears on your credit card, if using one)

Address: _____   E-mail: _____

City: _____   State: ____ Zip: _____

CC #: _____   MC VISA AMEX DISC Exp. _____

Tel.: _____   Signature _____

Special Value. Get the Set!

If purchased separately, Dick B.'s 14 titles would normally sell for US$256.30, plus Shipping and Handling (S&H). Using this Order Form, you may purchase sets of all 14 titles for **only US$199.95 per set**, plus US$25.00 for S&H (USPS Priority Mail).

Please mail this Order Form, along with your check or money order, to: Dick B., c/o Good Book Publishing Co., P.O. Box 837, Kihei, HI 96753-0837. Please make your check or money order payable to "**Dick B.**" in U.S. dollars drawn on a U.S. bank.